Jesus and Woman

JESUS
AND
WOMAN

An exciting discovery
of what he offered her

LISA SERGIO

EPM PUBLICATIONS, INC.

Published by EPM Publications, Inc.
McLean, Virginia, 1975

ISBN 0-914440-44-6
Library of Congress Catalog Card Number: 75-4365
Copyright © by Lisa Sergio
All Rights Reserved
Printed in the United States of America

Book and Jacket Designed
by Anne Hanger

For Adelaide H. Cabaniss

Acknowledgments

The title of this book could well suggest that the author is a Biblical scholar or one well versed in theology. Having no claim to such qualifications it has been my good fortune to receive support from those who possess what I lack. Thus, I am indebted to Rabbi William Seaman of Washington, D.C., to Dr. Leonard Swidler, Professor of Catholic Thought at Temple University, to Mrs. Emory Ross, for many years deeply involved with United Church Women, for the benefit of their careful reading of the manuscript and their suggestions for its improvement. The implicit significance of the relationship of Jesus to the women of his day has intrigued and interested me for a long time. That the result of researching this subject and of thinking about it for several years is now between covers is due in great measure to the encouragement of two dear and erudite friends: Dr. Eugene Exman, at one time my editor for another book, and Dr. John Anschutz, now Rector Emeritus of Christ Church Episcopal, Georgetown, Washington D.C. To merely say that I thank them is to make a vast understatement, as I hope they realize.

I am particularly happy that the publisher and editor of JESUS AND WOMAN should be a woman, Evelyn P. Metzger, who with her distinguished pediatrician husband, Dr. Arthur Metzger, has shown me a lively example of a partnership of man and woman, deriving its equality from their diversities. In vastly different ways I am grateful to them both. Others who have me in their debt include Heidi Shippee and Jane Currier, of EPM Publishing Company and Linda Stowe who, in an age of copying machines, can persuade the most recalcitrant to operate perfectly.

Finally the comments on the whole book by which three friends have honored me, Dr. Margaret Mead, Dr. Leon Salzman and the Rt. Rev. Paul Moore, Jr. have made me feel both proud and humble and, of course, immensely grateful.

Contents

1

A Partnership of Equals

In this second half of our century woman's demand for equality with man is no longer, as it once was, the cry of a few daring feminists of the Western world striving for an impossible goal. It is a voice heard around the earth. It is a call to action, drawing response from women who still toil from dawn to dusk in the rice paddies of India or in the fields of Africa, from women in the teeming cities of Japan or in the sea-washed villages of Oceania, from the women of Latin America too long kept in subjugation, from women in ancient Mediterranean and Middle Eastern lands, where veiled faces are disappearing. It is a response growing in breadth, rising in pitch and increasingly heeded as well as heard.

Woman's demand for equality has the power potential of a movement that can change the course of history by adding a new dimension—the feminine dimension—to the conduct of human affairs after thousands of years of male domination. The number of men who recognize that the world is moving towards almost certain disaster is swelling day by day, all over the globe. They concede that humanity's scale of values must be changed at the point where power is generated and policy imposed, and not merely within governments. An unprecedented and compelling influence must be brought into the management of human affairs, capable of carrying weight where power takes shape and where

1

decisions are made as to how and where it shall be used. Such an influence can only be the influence of woman because, in a bisexual world, she is man's only peer, even if millenia of history have seen her treated as his inferior. She must, however, become man's equal partner, and not merely his equal in the sense that he accepts her on his own terms in a society tailored to his traditional supremacy. She must become his equal in a partnership of equals. If woman is to play her full role she has no alternative to making this her goal.

The strength of any partnership lies in the diversity of its partners, whose different attributes, complementing each other, contribute to the formation of a complete, or more nearly complete, whole. Being equal is not synonymous with being identical. Nature itself, in the act of procreation, offers the perfect example of a partnership of equals. Although obviously not identical, each partner is nonetheless identically necessary to ensure the continuity of the species. Totally interdependent in their creative act, the partners are in no way interchangeable; neither can they successfully imitate one another. A similar partnership of minds has now become indispensable to ensure the continuity of society. One must wonder why at no time in history has any great leader, concerned with the welfare of humanity, seemed to have recognized that the physiological partnership of the sexes needed to be complemented by an intellectual one.

Had any such leader, Christian or not, rising to the fore since the advent of the common era, looked into the Gospels, he would have found that Jesus of Nazareth less than twenty centuries ago perceived the need for a partnership of male and female minds at the helm of human society. Although Jesus did not spell this out word for word in his teaching, his manner of treating woman demonstrated his belief in her equality, and the implications of his personal encounters with several individual women pointed to the role he expected her to play as the equal partner of man.

The Gospel narratives are the legacy of four Jewish men— Matthew, a tax collector for the Romans; Mark, a Jerusalemite whose mother was a property owner; Luke, a physician; and John, a Galilean fisherman—brought up to look upon woman as chattel. Because in their accounts of Jesus' life they treat woman as an equal person, one must assume that it was Jesus who converted them to this attitude. Indeed, the most significant encounters between the Nazarene and one or another of several women are reported in such detail as to leave little room for doubt that the Evangelists' highlighting of woman in each case was intentional.

In those days, not only was woman legally defined as chattel, but many even questioned if she possessed a soul. When ready for marriage the girl was bartered between her father—or male guardian—and the prospective husband, rarely with her consent even though this was theoretically required. The man could divorce his wife, but no way existed for the wife to divorce her husband. Females were rarely tutored or taught the Torah, although they were obliged to obey its negative commands. They were legally barred from giving testimony or appearing in court. It was only while a woman was raising her sons that she achieved authority and prestige, in obvious contradiction to her basic condition as an inferior. Until her boys turned thirteen, the Jewish mother had full control over them, and by the time they were placed under paternal rule she was to have implanted in them their religion, their ethics and the values by which they were to live. After that she resumed her chattel status.

This was the background of discrimination against which Jesus not only permitted women to join his fellowship, but actually invited them to do so. Throughout his life, even as he publicly decried the hypocrisy he saw in many prevailing laws and customs, he publicly displayed his respect and affection for woman and his concern for the soul he knew her to possess. In the end, his support of woman as a person was undoubtedly counted by his enemies among the allegedly revolutionary acts that led to his death on Mount Golgotha.

The status of today's woman, particularly in the Western world and in other societies patterned after it, has made gigantic forward strides even though it falls short of full equality. In terms of numbers and of her recognized consequence as a political and economic factor, woman has the potential influence needed to steer the world away from its present course. Unless there is a drastic change of direction, humanity will come face to face with annihilation in a gigantic holocaust or will continue to move inexorably towards extinction of life in the polluted environment of a planet whose resources are being recklessly depleted while its population grows at a lethal rate.

However, could these trends be arrested without radical change, we would still be confronted with world-wide agitation laced with violence, the price of man's failure to heed the cry and to meet the needs of that vast segment of humanity already afflicted by the dehumanizing effects of enslavement by technology. For thousands of years the male wielders of power have shown too little concern for the rights of the human person and even less for those of the mind and spirit. Woman must make it her task to cause these rights to become the undergirding of a bold and world-wide pattern of society in which freedom, justice and compassion are as much the requisites of life as oxygen is of breathing. For an undertaking of such magnitude she must be man's full partner in the management of human affairs, not because she is a better person than he, but because she is different. She is naturally endowed with certain qualifications which man possesses in lesser measure or does not possess at all. These are the qualifications or attributes on which Jesus cast light in his remarkable encounters with certain average women of his time and society.

Intellectual and psychological differences exist between man and woman to the same extent that there are physiological differences between them and all are of equally vital importance. Interestingly enough, however, whereas a normal woman does not regard these physiological differences as demeaning to her dignity or status, the mere suggestion that there are also certain differences of intellect and psychology between her and man arouses strong feminist resentment.

The logical fact is that if woman had nothing different to contribute to the management of human affairs from what it already receives from man, her participation would be neither interesting nor necessary. Socially concerned men, now aware of the nature of the forces by which humanity is being driven towards disaster, also realize their own inadequacies in trying to control them. Likewise they are beginning to perceive that woman possesses attributes capable of compensating for these inadequacies in meeting the challenges of our age. They are increasingly supporting her claim to equality because she is different from them and, by virtue of her differences, indispensable to the survival of society. Admittedly or implicitly, today's enlightened and sophisticated man seeks an equal partner among the enlightened and sophisticated women, rejecting those who merely strive to imitate him.

Delving into the Gospels for this appraisal, one is struck by the fact that almost every time Jesus broke new ground in his ministry, a woman was cast in a primary role at his side, as though he wished to highlight her importance by linking her with an act which he had never performed before. Ten such occasions can be singled out, each involving a different woman who, in no way unique as an individual, is typical of many other women of all time. Five of them are not even known to us by their names, but only by their condition: a sick woman, a Samaritan, an adulteress, a generous woman and a penniless widow. The other five are Mary, the mother of Jesus; Mary of Magdala, the woman cured of possession by the devils; Mary and Martha, sisters of Lazarus; and Claudia Procula, wife of Pontius Pilate and the only one who most probably had never seen the Nazarene.

In reconstructing and analyzing these episodes one discovers how, by implication, each of them illustrates one or more facets of woman's role as the partner of man. They also provide the answer to a question which can hardly fail to arise in the mind of anyone who sees how sharply Jesus broke with tradition in his recognition of woman's equality. The question is the following: since Jesus went so far as to liberate the women of his circle from subjugation, treating them as disciples, why did he not give them a part in the mission to be carried on after his death? The male disciples were told specifically to travel to far places, preach his gospel to Jew and Gentile, remit sins, heal the sick and draw into the ranks whoever, rejecting violence and hate, accepted his doctrine of love and forgiveness. But nowhere do the Gospels relate that he gave an assignment to the women, an omission which seems inconsistent with his daily dealings with women as well as with the very spirit of his teaching.

The answer is that Jesus did give woman a commission, even as he gave one to man, but he did not specifically put hers into direct words. Instead, it was in the course of each woman's encounter with him that she was shown a part if not all of the role he wished her to play. And although the encounters and their implications were individual, their fundamental significance is timeless and universal. Indeed, as soon as we view these various episodes as parts of a whole, the facets of woman's role which each implies fall into place like the pieces of a puzzle. They develop a picture of universal woman as the equal partner of universal man.

Jesus was a past-master in the use of symbolism, at times to clarify the meaning of what he was teaching, at others to challenge the perspicacity of his listeners. The means he used to apprise his male and female disciples of their respective missions are fascinatingly symbolic of the differences in the intrinsic nature of the missions themselves. As the Gospels tell, the task assigned to the men was one of 'outreach'. They were to go out into the world to build a society patterned after his teachings and to propagate love and brotherhood among enemies as well as friends. The women's task, instead, was one of 'inreach.' They were to restore or to build those moral and social foundations which must lie at the heart of each and every person if human society is to stand secure. The foundations of a building are obviously concealed from view; thus Jesus, symbolically, gave woman her commission wrapped in subtle implications. Likewise symbolic of the difference between 'reaching out' and 'reaching in' were the means by which certain men—the twelve disciples—and certain women—those with whom he established a personal and direct relationship—were given enlightenment for their respective tasks.

Thus we learn that on a certain day when the twelve male disciples were gathered together in Jerusalem, a flame descending suddenly in their midst and blinding them for a time by its light, endowed their minds with knowledge of such depth and breadth as to transcend all human limitations. These once simple men were made capable of so affecting the minds of those who thereafter heard them speak or saw them act that, accepting the doctrine of the Nazarene, their actions and their way of life were transformed.

Although present, the female disciples did not receive the gift of tongues, for they did not need to have at their command a sophisticated means of mass communication. Their need was for an inner light by which to see their inner selves. They needed to perceive their own natural gifts as sources of power to be developed and put to use as instruments of 'inreach' by means of which to change human motivation. Therefore the women received inner light not from a flame descending from on high, but from one sparked in their individual consciences by what the Nazarene said and did in the brief moment of their personal encounters with him.

To perceive the psychological climate in which Jesus chose to touch and transform these ten women, is to see the modern relevance of these episodes because human psychology has not changed with the passing of the ages and people still react in similar manner to similar situations. The setting and the circumstances that create a given psychological climate, even if they are part of a society two thousand years removed from us, have modern parallels which quickly come to mind as we reconstruct the original situations related in the Gospel.

Although the authenticity of the Gospels and their historical validity continue to be challenged, the fact remains that humanity has known about the life and teachings of Jesus only from the records of his four contemporaries, Matthew, Mark, Luke and John. Christianity, as a faith and a way of life, and Christendom, as a structure to organize the practice of it, have made their way through twenty centuries of history solely on the strength of the Gospels. Despite some fifteen hundred years of scholarly and often adverse studies of these texts, not only has the substance of what Jesus taught remained intact, but it has also been adopted by such great non-Christian leaders as India's Mahatma Gandhi, to mention but one of many. Furthermore, certain of Christianity's basic tenets, although drastically shorn of their religious and ethical framework, have been absorbed into communist or Marxist ideology, a fact which percolates through the ongoing dialogue between Christian and Marxist scholars.

The Gospel narratives make clear the extent to which Jesus was shocked by the declining morality, the hypocrisy, the lack of love and brotherhood he found among his people. Inveighing against these sins, he addressed himself to the men, but from his efforts to make the women conscious of their part in society, we must deduce his awareness of the responsibility which woman had not adequately fulfilled. Since every man is born of woman and since the initial upbringing of every Jewish male had been left to his mother, it stands to reason that, if a male-governed society showed signs of deterioration, mothers could not eschew their share of blame. Likewise, if a society's moral standards were to be restored or reformed, the first step in this direction would have to be taken by mothers having authority to implant these standards in their sons. Those sons, in turn, becoming adults, would have the will to uplift the standards of society as a whole. Therefore, motherhood marks the beginning of the partnership of men and women in the shaping of society. If we assume, as we must, that Jesus saw this clearly, we must also assume that his determination to compel his own society to treat woman as the equal of man meant he saw that woman has a variety of contributions to make to society. He did not limit the mandate he gave her by implication to the role of a character-forming mother. Indeed, deeply as we may examine the Gospels, we find no sign that Jesus intended woman to be confined to the interests and activities of her household or even of her community. Woman's world was to be as wide as the world which man saw as his own.

Look upon the Nazarene as one will—awaited Messiah, Son of God, prophet, man of vision, psychic, revolutionary or peacemaker

—his evaluation of the power of woman is as timely, fresh and realistic today, in our threatened nuclear-conscious world, as it was when he talked in easy parables to the simple people gathered around him in the serene countryside of Galilee.

The first of the ten encounters, linking Jesus to woman with transcendent significance, occurs in Jerusalem between the boy of twelve and Mary, a loving mother who has sought him in anguish through the city streets. The last is between the man of thirty-three, who has overcome the ordeal of death, and another Mary, a loving follower who, in anguish, has sought his body in a tomb. The first is tangible and worldly. The last is spiritual, visible to human eyes but intangible to human hands. The first reveals the glimmer of a light to come. The last reflects the radiance of a light without end.

2

Words in the Temple

The long caravan of Jewish pilgrims, going home to Nazareth after celebrating the Passover in Jerusalem, radiated gladness as men, women and boys tramped over the curving roads which the Romans had carved out of the harsh Judaean countryside. Frequently breaking into song, neither young nor old appeared to mind the prospect of the long trek ahead of them.

One obvious exception was a young woman walking beside her husband, without song on her lips or smile in her eyes. The man, older than she, looked back frequently, as though expecting someone to join them. It was the unaccountable absence of their young son, Jesus, that was causing so much concern to Joseph and Mary of Nazareth on what should have been a joyful homeward journey. The boy had just completed his twelfth year. For the first time, his parents had taken him to Jerusalem. Had he not always been so obedient and considerate, they might have worried less about his absence. But it was not like him to fail to do as he was told.

When the sun began to set on the first day's march and their son had not appeared, they turned back to look for him. Walking until dawn to reach Jerusalem, they walked again all day through the city, inquiring at markets and in countless other places, but all to no avail. The next morning, as a last resort, they made their way back to the temple.

Built by Herod where Solomon's original structure had once stood, and still quite new, the vast place of worship was an arresting sight. The tall pillars cast long shadows on the sunlit pavement, the white walls set off the gates of gold that vied for splendor with arches and columns patterned against blue skies. The temple was not only a place of worship, but also the fountainhead of Mosaic learning, the court of law, a debating forum and a general meeting place for all Jews.

Suddenly, from a distance, they caught sight of the boy in the enclosure where scripture was being taught. Seated among the Rabbis, he was speaking while the wise men listened. Startled, Mary and Joseph paused outside the holy precinct. Then, leaving Mary in the Women's Court, Joseph walked towards Jesus, beckoned to him and lead him back to his mother. Reproachfully, she addressed him saying: "My son, why have you treated us like this? Your father and I have been searching for you in great anxiety." But Jesus, looking surprised, answered her with questions of his own: "What made you search for me? Did you not know that I was to be in my Father's house?" Not quite understanding what the boy meant, his parents exchanged puzzled glances but said nothing more, convinced as they both were that his surprise was genuine and that he had not intended to disobey.

As they all traveled back to Nazareth, happy to be reunited, her son's unusual remark was uppermost in Mary's consciousness but, not mentioning it again, "she kept it in her heart and pondered it." According to Jewish custom, she had been fully responsible for the upbringing of her son up to that time. Consequently, in the temple, her husband had let her reprimand their child, because it was from his mother that he had learned obedience and to her that he was still accountable. Upon returning to Nazareth, however, he would be counted among the adult men and formally out of his mother's charge. He would be apprenticed to his father in the carpenter's trade, schooled in the scriptures by the Rabbis and taken to sit with Joseph in the synagogue, instead of with Mary, behind the women's screen, as he had done for uncounted Sabbaths through his childhood years.

Looking back upon those times through our twentieth century eyes, a paradox appears before us. Although the women of Israel were legally defined as chattel, totally subjected to the will of their men, as mothers they were given authority in the raising of their children. While girls remained the mother's charge until they were married off, boys were under maternal control only until they turned thirteen. By that time, the mother was expected to have developed the character and personality of the nation's future citizens and leaders in accordance with the religious beliefs and moral precepts dictated to Moses by the Lord Jehovah, and handed down through the centuries from generation to generation. Thus, in a temporary way conditioned by the age and sex of her offspring, the Jewish mother attained a unique level of equality with her spouse. The physical partnership of male and female that had brought a new child into the world was transformed into an intellectual and moral partnership of man and woman responsible for bringing a completely developed personality into society.

To observe the actions and reactions of almost any adult in any type of society usually means to discover a great deal about his childhood and particularly about the mother who brought him up. Although little or nothing is known about Jesus as an adolescent and a youth, nevertheless to observe him as a man in the three years of his public adult life means to discover Mary—a young mother, wise with the wisdom of the ages—as she journeyed with him through his first twelve years. The responsibility which fell to her lot because she was the mother of a boy was obviously accepted by Mary with joyful dedication, sublimated by her mysticism and by her inner certainty that he was "different" from other children his age.

Ever since mankind has been on earth, every newborn has had to learn how to eat, to walk, to speak. Likewise every newborn mind has had to learn how to think, to choose, to reason and to act. By love and instinct every normal mother helps her child's body to grow healthy, active and strong. But not so readily or instinctively does she take on the task of awakening the soul and mind of that same child. While it is not likely that Mary was a strict parent, we can well imagine her bending every effort to develop in her firstborn a faith so deep, a character so strong and self-discipline so firmly rooted that the full-grown man would be prepared for whatever calling might be his. Her intuition must have told her that his calling would not be ordinary, even if she could hardly have forseen how uniquely great and ultimately tragic it would be.

Although he too, quite normally, learnt his first lessons at his mother's knee, these did not reflect book-learning, since Mary herself had had none. Rather, it was through the faith in which she had been raised that she made him realize that God was a living presence, whose voice spoke to every human conscience and whose commands were to take precedence over those imparted by man. Naturally, then, Jesus had been surprised by her reproach in the Temple, because he expected her to know, without his having had to tell her, that, in staying behind, he had merely heeded the voice of God. Likewise, Mary must have taught him early to share what he had with those who had less than he, and thus caused him to notice at once the inequities resulting from human greed. His world was not so very different from ours. Some people gorged themselves or were wasteful while others starved; virtue did not always triumph over sin; poverty of spirit often came in the company of material want, while little was done by society to assuage the hurt of either. His world, like ours today, was one in which too many powerful men claiming to rule in the name of God and for the good of the people, were betraying the Almighty and deceiving the populace in order to serve their own ends.

It it probable that Jesus had his first encounters with the seamier realities of life as he ran errands for his father in the narrow streets and crowded market places of Nazareth, or made deliveries to wealthy customers. On occasion, the young apprentice must have come home distressed by what he had seen, heart and mind in rebellion against established power. His mother, understanding him, must have let him express his feelings as the spirit moved him, not realizing that he would dedicate himself to righting these wrongs, whatever the cost. In fact, raised as Jesus was in a conservative and circumscribed religious milieu, it is apparent that certain of his revolutionary teachings were a reaction to his background. His attacks on hypocrisy and formalism were probably spurred by certain of the vacuous practices that hemmed him in as a child, and his concern for women by the repression to which he saw them subjected. For instance, after the death of Joseph, Jesus certainly saw how diminished was the status of his mother in the community merely because she was widowed and had no more sons to raise. He must have understood then how such discrimination against capable and thoughtful women deprived Jewish society of an element vital to its progress and, therefore, from the start of his ministry or perhaps even before, he treated women as complete and equal persons and attracted them into his following. At the same time, however, his mother's steadfast clinging to a traditionalism which he grew to abhor, must have given him deep respect for her refusal to compromise with her own convictions. Like her, Jesus never compromised with the dictates of his conscience, his principles or his love for humanity.

Mary's twentieth century counterparts as young mothers, possess the same maternal authority she exercised in her time, with the difference that Mary was required to use it, whereas modern mothers are free to surrender it to other influences as they frequently choose to do. Nevertheless, women who do understand that the shaping of their children's minds and characters must proceed hand in hand with the building of their bodies, must certainly be aware of the positive effect they can have in determining the quality and the values of a society of which their children will eventually constitute the citizenry and possibly the leadership.

Moreover, as the struggle for woman's equality continues to expand, today's young mother can serve the cause of feminism much more effectively by keeping the minds of her growing sons free from the anti-feminist prejudices in which their elders were reared, than she can by her loudest protests against male domination. If she believes that a partnership of equal men and women in every field of endeavor is the ideal goal to strive for, as a mother she has the power to make that partnership a working reality in her own family and thereby cause her sons and daughters to accept it as a normal way of life.

The lessons to be drawn from what Mary did are ageless. For instance, the passing of centuries has in no way reduced the need for men and women to "keep things in their heart and ponder them" as she did, before speaking or jumping to conclusions. In our age of mass communications, when words rush out like torrents in all directions, frequently doing as much damage to those who speak as to those who listen, the habit of 'pondering' is one that every child should be helped to acquire. It is, in fact, a deplorable aspect of modern life that a vast number of children, caught in a web of adult restlessness and tensions, frequently suffer the consequences of decisions made without enough reflection by their elders. The ambience of innumerable homes, where constant noise prevails, is not only a deterent to reflection, but it is also a serious threat to the personality of children on their way to adulthood. While a certain amount of noise may well have become unavoidable in modern society, much of it is needlessly due to blaring radios, stereos, television sets and musical instruments powered more by electricity than by human talent. This clangor defiles the sound waves reaching human ears, doing as much harm to the vital organs of hearing as it hampers our thinking process. Also appalling is the potential damage done to young minds by ideas, suggestions or facts, some good and some evil, conveyed and hurled at them by mechanical carriers, when they are still too inexperienced to know which to accept and which to bar.

Parents and teachers, but mothers particularly, who are reluctant to protect children by policing their lives, must at least arm even the very young with the habit of thinking before acting and with the courage to turn to their elders for support, regardless of who or what may have them under pressure. No better weapon than the habit of counting ten and thinking, can the young be given as protection against tempters trying to lure them into trouble. Most of today's juvenile offenders or those who are already delinquents, show a shocking incapacity to think beyond the range of the guns they carry or the fists they swing. They have never been taught to think, either at home or at school. Thought, the process that keeps civilization moving, is one that, like walking or talking, must be learned by stimulation.

Haste, like noise, also deters thinking and reflection. In Mary's household, one may be sure that there was no rushing and no haste and that the child Jesus was not exposed to their effect, for never does a sense of haste or pressure emanate from his words and actions as a man. True, in his time the pace of life was slow, but, as the Gospel shows, Jesus could act and react with speed while others procrastinated, aware as he was that haste and speed are not one and the same thing. Haste is taking less time than necessary, whereas speed is doing the necessary without wasting time. While the latter may be vital, the former can be lethal. Knowing how to differentiate between them is a matter of discernment which, in turn, is a practice to be acquired in childhood and made to grow in sophistication as the person grows. If we observe the Nazarene as he travels with his friends, addresses a crowd, responds to a cry for help or rebukes a malevolent challenger, the hasteless timing of whatever he does or says pays tribute to his discernment. Also, whoever approached him in a state of anxiety, beset by real or imaginary fears, was immediately soothed by the unhurried quality of his response that gradually transformed tensions into serene self-confidence.

Our century, in fact, suffers from the deification of haste. What began as a characteristic of the New World, having spread to the Old, is an ailment starting to affect even the slow-moving East. While nothing good or evil can ever be tracked down to any one single cause, haste is a force destined to have an increasingly negative effect as human society becomes increasingly dependent on science and technology. Looking at science, as we see it in the 70's, we find that most, if not all, the scientists to whom we owe the major discoveries and technological developments that are transforming our world, were youths growing to maturity at a time when incessant noise and constant haste had little part in life or education. Today's children, from whose ranks must come tomorrow's scientists and technologists, raised as they are at the mercy of mechanisms devised for speed, scarcely realize that every such mechanism results from the patient expenditure of endless time by those who brought it forth. Moreover, our computerized societies need scores of individuals trained for patience and precision, since the computer has an awesome way of magnifying the least of human errors or inaccuracies. Computers are incompatible with haste despite their time-saving capacities.

While haste endangers life or all too easily takes its toll of limb, it also strikes at the core of three of life's essentials: love, justice and freedom. This is a fact which every child can be taught to understand and to remember. Love rarely survives the ill-effects of hasty words or hastily considered actions. Justice, quite obviously, must suffer whenever a judgment—be it public or private—is made without a full evaluation of every element capable of affecting its fairness, regardless of how time-consuming the process. Freedom—individual or collective as the case may be—is almost always lost when those who claim to cherish it do not take time to protect it. History shows that, at some juncture, the collective freedom of any people can be confronted by the might of a government or of other forces determined to destroy that freedom to satisfy their lust for power and more power. Where people are still free, the voice of public opinion, clearly expressed, can defeat these forces. But, as we have seen happen, if a majority of vocal individuals speak hastily and without reflecting, or under the spell of an emotional appeal, their collective voice may betray their personal belief and make them slaves.

Interestingly enough, emotional mass appeals were not unknown even in the days of Jesus. Then as now, their objective might have been good or evil. The preaching of John the Baptist, for instance, illustrates a highly successful appeal to mass emotions for a good purpose. Emerging from the wilderness, the Baptist attracted large crowds by his merciless tongue-lashings of sinners to whom he promised salvation in return for true repentance. On the contrary, the scene in Jerusalem's Tower of Antonia, where Jesus was on trial before an ignorant mob, is an example of mass emotions aroused with horrifying success for the most evil of intentions. The habitual crowd of loafers, packed into the place of judgment on the morning which Christians know as Good Friday, were galvanized into a state of frenzy by the enemies of Jesus concealed in their midst. Even as Pontius Pilate was declaring the prisoner innocent, the mob shouted "Crucify Jesus! Set Barabbas free!". When frenzy began to verge on violence, the mob prevailed, and justice was paid off with a mere washing of hands.

One may well pause to wonder what Mary, the Nazarene's mother, may have thought of that fanatical mass of men and youths if, in her advancing years, her mind ever turned back to that appalling day. She must have told herself that, had those males been raised by mothers willing to teach them to respect truth, to recognize the voice of their own conscience and to use their minds to think, the evil provocations of her son's enemies would have gone for naught. How timely for the mothers of today's young delinquents would such a reflection prove to be!

Where, better than in his own home, can a child begin to place a value on those realities of life that will ultimately shape his character? Who, better than a mother, can teach a child to use that most marvelous of tools, the human mind? Who can help him to develop character and make it bear the most rewarding fruits? Who will teach him about honesty and truth, about moral values and how to scale them above the material ones? How to strive for perfection in whatever he undertakes? Who will open his eyes to justice, to freedom and to love? Who will guide him to seek the presence of God within himself? This magnificent process of spiritual and intellectual discovery should move forward as naturally under a mother's sustaining mind as does that of discovering how to walk, or eat or talk. But, whereas any normal young mother is fascinated and delighted by the experience of seeing her child take its first steps, brandish a spoon as though it were a weapon of conquest, or transform sounds into words, she often seems awed and baffled by the challenge of intellectual shoots ready to burst into bloom. Millions of mothers are surrendering to television screens, nursery schools, classroom teacher, scout master and even to the neighborhood gang their responsibility for the healthy growth of a young mind. Modern parents have been told that, at all costs, children must 'identify' with their peers lest, by being different, they become outcasts. Many mothers adopt this prescription only to discover too late that it should have been labeled "Deadly Poison, Beware!"

To enumerate the consequences which have already resulted from woman's abdication of this essential and most rewarding role would be to state the obvious. The escalation of delinquency and crime among the very young in a society we like to think of as progressive and advanced, may well suffice as an example. The remedy for the evil of lawlessness will come not from the police, the school or even the church, but from the home—a place which normally is, and always has been, what a woman decides to make it.

One aspect of Mary's task that cannot have been easy for her, was having to deal with a precocious and highly intelligent boy, who rebelled against hypocrisy in any form. We learn from the Gospels that Jesus found plenty of it to combat without restraint when the time was ripe for him to do so. But had he not grown up in a home where candor and mutual trust were evidently sovereign, his innate passion for sincerity and truth might have been stunted at the outset. Most children are more observant than their parents give them credit for. Whatever is untrue, whatever reveals a double standard of parental behavior or shows a discrepancy between adult teaching and adult practice rarely escapes them. Eventually, the children too will take what, judging by the example of their elders, appears to be the easiest way—more frequently than not a road paved with hypocrisy and hard to abandon in mid-course. One can be certain that neither Joseph nor Mary offered their boy any such temptation.

Selfless and understanding of what was best for her son as Mary must certainly have been, she was nonetheless human and when Jesus had left Nazareth and was totally involved in his mission, she could not resist the urge to try to get him back. It was a mistake, as she soon discovered. It was a Sabbath and Jesus, entering a synagogue, healed a man with a withered arm. The Pharisees, having witnessed the event, plotted to kill the healer. Jesus moved on, but the crowd followed him and he cured many among them. Again the doctors of the law and the Pharisees were after him trying to trap him, but he silenced them even as he continued to address the multitude that would not leave him. Someone approached him saying: "Your mother and your brothers are here; they want to speak to you."

Perhaps sensing the perils that stalked her son and yielding to the pressures of his brothers who abhorred his non-conformism and his passion for reform, Mary had come from Nazareth to the lake of Galilee when she heard that Jesus was there. She was determined to talk to him and, no doubt, persuade him to return home. Jesus turned to the man who had brought the message and said, "Who is my mother? Who are my brothers?", then pointing to the disciples, added, "Here are my mother and my brothers. Whoever does the will of my heavenly Father is my brother, my sister, my mother."

His words had the ring of a rejection that must have angered his brothers and deeply pained his mother, and he refused to see them. It may well have been his way of reminding Mary, and through her all mothers, that he was now an adult, a responsible man bent on a mission, and out of her hands. Realizing as he certainly did, that she was aware of his enemies and afraid for his life, he was also reminding her that he was fully able to face his own problems since she, herself, had taught him to face all things squarely.

Regardless of this episode, Jesus did not cease to be a loving son. Among the last words that passed his lips, as he was dying on the cross, were those which placed his mother in the care of John, the youngest and most cherished of his own disciples. Even in the dreadfulness of the end he did not forget the tenderness of the beginning of which Mary had been a vital and intrinsic part.

3

Wine in the Water Jars

In the days of Jesus a wedding was a public event in which the entire community participated, a custom that still survives in many parts of the world. Even if the couple's families were of small substance, the banquet was liberally laden with food and wine and formality vanished as soon as feasting began. Guests were usually of two kinds: the kin and friends who were personally invited and came bearing gifts, including food, and the towns-people, tacitly bidden, some of whom brought small tokens in appreciation of the good fun and fare they were about to enjoy.

The little town of Cana in Galilee was filled with the excitement of such a wedding. Mary, the mother of Jesus, who was related to the groom, had gone to Cana a few days earlier to help the women with the preparations. Joseph, her husband, had been dead some time and Jesus, now head of the family had been absent for several weeks for reasons which Mary had only discovered through third persons. Her son, she was told, had been baptized by John on the banks of the river Jordan but had withdrawn immediately into the wilderness to meditate in solitude. He had not returned to Nazareth, but she had received word that he would be a groomsman at the wedding. This was making her extremely happy.

Cana was a pleasant little town, laid out on the descent of a hill on the caravan route that made its way through valleys, climbed hills and skirted towns and villages, going inland from the Mediterranean coast to the imperial city of Tiberias on the Sea of Galilee. Cana's houses stood fairly close to one another, sunning themselves on a slope among pomegranate groves and vineyards to which the gnarled and contorted trunks of olive trees added a strangely dramatic touch, their silvery-gray leaves quivering in the breeze like wafts of incense in a place of prayer. The bubbling springs concealed in the rich soil fed abundant water to fields stretched out like carpets of green. Come the warm season, a mass of brilliant flowers gowned the fields in patterns of dazzling beauty, so that "even Solomon in all his splendour was not attired like one of these."

Mary, who no doubt had helped at many a wedding, cannot have remembered any into which she had placed so much of her heart and soul as on this occasion at Cana. Because Jesus was coming she wanted everything to be perfect. Detached though he was from the mundane, he had, nonetheless, an observant eye from which no imperfection escaped. He had a feeling for beauty that made him come alive at the sight of it, in the creations of man as in those of nature.

The event, which always took place in the evening, proceeded according to ancient tradition. The bride was fetched from her parents' home by the town elders and a gathering of friends and relatives escorted her litter to the synagogue through streets lined with people tossing flowers and singing to the accompaniment of musicians who brought up the rear of the gay procession. Several of the bride's young attendants, virgins gowned in white, preceded the litter, carrying lighted oil lamps and chatting as they walked.

The groom, meanwhile, following his groomsmen who carried laurel branches with their lights, would be on his way to the synagogue by another route. Before reaching it, however, he would be met by the virgins who, holding their lamps aloft, had gone to find him as soon as they had left the bride under the marriage canopy.

From ancient times, when the maiden's quest for her loved one had been immortalized in poetry, each succeeding generation had faithfully observed the ancient ritual, walking in procession down countless streets in countless villages, singing his words: "I will rise now and go about the city; in the broadways I will seek him whom my soul loveth." The religious tying of the marriage knot was fraught with special pomp because the Jewish people looked upon every wedding as a re-welding of the bonds which, from time immemorial, had linked the Chosen People to their one God. For this reason a marriage was a community affair. Farmers left the fields and artisans their tools to don the special garment which men wore only for this occasion. First they would worship, then they would make merry.

After the ceremony Jesus and several of his disciples who were also groomsmen, scattered through the crowd. The music was lively, the wine well-aged, the fare well-spiced and the guests in a merry mood. As the evening wore on, Mary overheard the governor of the feast ask the chief steward if he had any further supply of wine. When she saw the steward shake his head, Mary realized that a lack of wine at that stage of the festivities would not only be a public humiliation for the groom, but might even start trouble. Her heart went out to the young man seated at the other end of the hall. She knew that something would have to be done, and done without delay. Obviously, her first thought was of her son, the kindest and most understanding person she had ever known.

When her eyes found him in the hall she threaded her way to where he stood and whispered: "They have no wine." Jesus, bending towards her, merely said: "Your concern is not mine, woman. My time has not yet come." The term 'woman' was an expression of regard to which Jesus' tone certainly added his customary warmth, but his words were nonetheless firm and final. Mary, adding no further word to her plea, turned to the servants, saying: "Do whatever he tells you to do." Then she mingled quickly with the guests, without losing sight of her son.

Almost at once Jesus told the water carriers, who were standing near their twenty-gallon water jars, to fill them full and, when he saw the water brim, he said: "Draw some and take it to the steward of the feast." Quickly the servants obeyed and the steward, amazed by the quality of the wine he was unexpectedly being asked to taste when he believed that none was available, rushed over to the groom exclaiming: "Everyone serves the best wine first, and waits until the guests have drunk freely before serving the poorer sort; but you have kept the best wine until now."

What happened then? Who told the gathering where the good wine had come from? It could have been Mary who gave it away by the look of pride in her face; it could have been one of the disciples, whose faith in the Master had suddenly been confirmed by the unexpected wonder; or it could have been the servants and it most likely was, since they were the only real witnesses to the amazing feat. At all events, as the fresh supply of wine went around the hall so did the news: Jesus of Nazareth, the carpenter, had changed water into wine! Commotion probably ensued, with some people pushing to get close to the miracle-maker, others trying to see him over a hedge of shoulders and those who were envious or disbelieving probably shaking their heads but holding their tongues.

No doubt, if Jesus had not reversed his first decision, nothing more serious would have occurred than his young relative's loss of face and perhaps some raising of voices on the part of those who, having already indulged, wanted more. But the miracle, of course, did far more than prevent these unpleasant consequences. By his own determination, this became the first public act of his ministry and a turning point in his life. For the benefit of others, Jesus chose to reveal the supernatural powers which he had stolidly refused to use for his own sake when a wily Satan, seeking him out while he meditated, fasting in the wilderness, persistently tried to tempt him to do so. At Cana, Jesus took a momentous and irreversible step in yielding to a woman's plea, thus telling all womankind to take to heart everything that his unprecedented act implied.

The implications were numerous and profoundly meaningful: the bringing forth of wine came in response to the altruism and sensitivity of a woman; the wine spared a young man a humiliation he had not deserved; Jesus found it important to not break up the happy mood of a wedding feast; the wine itself carried a particular social significance and the quality of it bespoke Jesus' belief in perfectionism even when none was expected or, even less, required.

When Mary suddenly wondered what to do about the wine and spoke to Jesus, it is conceivable that she hoped he might know of a place where wine could be found in the nearby countryside, since he had just been traveling through that area. Her request does not necessarily suggest that she was asking him for a miracle, although the history of her people was replete with them. On the contrary, the suggestion that a supernatural act was required came from Jesus himself whose words "my time has not yet come" carried a prophetic overtone, implying that "his time" would come in due course. However, it was Mary's thoughtfulness in her concern for the young groom that compelled him to reverse his decision and, for her sake, publicly initiate his mission to humanity at that wedding.

The very simplicity of Mary's plea must have helped to change her son's mind. She used only four words—"they have no wine" —whose unadorned realism conveyed the urgency of her request as well as her own certainty that it would stand on its merits without further explanation. Mary must have known by instinct that a strong plea is weakened by unsolicited detail and its urgency impaired by wordiness. When next she spoke it was to make an implicit declaration of faith in her son's judgment, and here again her choice of words cannot have escaped him. She told the servants: "Do whatever he tells you to do." Just as reasonably she might have said: "If he tells you to do something, do it" but there was no place for 'ifs' in Mary's faith.

Not only her son Jesus, but any person having power to grant a request, then as at any time, is more likely to be persuaded by the pleader's faith in that power than by detailed arguments to press the case. Maybe this is an implicit lesson which Jesus intended all women to learn from Mary, whose problem he resolved that evening with such unexpected munificence.

Since the objective of Mary's concern was to save a young man from humiliation and her son achieved it for her, we must assume that Jesus measured the importance of saving the groom's pride by Mary's scale of values rather than by the one he had made his own. We know, for instance, how on a later occasion, he cast aside the normally accepted standards of man's dignity and pride to firmly proclaim: "When a man hits you on the cheek, offer him the other cheek too." These contrasting positions may seem to reflect a double standard of judgment, but in reality they both express the Nazarene's constant and overriding concern with the human condition of the individual person. His actions say that no human value is an absolute, but that each must be viewed and assessed in the light of the conditions which affect it. That evening at Cana, the groom had just attained a higher social standing as a married man, his rise in status being a significant event in Jewish tradition, carrying influence into his future. Obviously, this should not have been demeaned by such a trivial matter as miscalculating the amount of wine required for the feast. If what we read into this is a lesson in how to evaluate a human need and how to meet it justly, then we can hardly escape the conclusion that his example was directed specifically to woman, since it was a woman's perception of a need and of its urgency that persuaded Jesus to perform his first miracle.

Apparently, the festivities had reached a crucial point when the wine ran out and the mood that was gay might easily have become unpleasant or even angry. By preserving the gaiety, Jesus chose to highlight the importance he attached to the act of marriage, which is a new seedling of society, even as a birth is a new seedling of life.

Particularly significant to woman is the fact that Jesus initiated his public ministry at a wedding because, in all societies, this is the starting point of her social partnership with man and, among the Jews, it was the one public function in which woman participated on a more or less equal footing with man. Here, too, Jesus revealed his superhuman power in addition to his already recognized human gifts, as if to indicate that the power of things spiritual has a vital role in what must be a union of minds as well as bodies. And, again, the implication seems to be that it is a woman's special responsibility to bring the spiritual element into the marriage partnership.

We know, of course that Jesus performed many and far more striking miracles after the one at Cana. Indeed, changing water into wine could not match, for dramatic quality, the restoring of sight to the blind, of sanity to the possessed, of wholesomeness to the leper or of life to the dead. But it was the first miracle he performed and, like all first steps onto a new road, it was taken with hesitation and did not have the dimension of a great stride. But this too, has its symbolic meaning, since it is a reminder that he who would rise to great heights must first get off the ground. For modern woman, whose feminism aims for the highest level of partnership with man, it is an invitation to follow the Nazarene's example by starting her upward drive from solid ground. It seems to signify that, first of all, she must come to know her own self, recognizing the full worth of her special assets, so that her initial step towards complete equality with man will carry with it the best of her unique contribution to their joint endeavors.

In all societies, and to this day, it has always been a woman's task, sometimes her serious problem as well, to prepare, if not also to provide, food for those around her. On the whole, womankind has regarded this as drudgery and as one more indication of the inferior condition to which man has always sought to relegate her. At Cana, however, we find Jesus initiating a ministry that was to be supremely spiritual at a very mundane affair which his miracle made all the more enjoyable for the guests. Indeed, we know that he liked to dine not only with his friends but with all sorts of people who came his way, and when he multiplied the loaves and fishes to feed a multitude, his care was that those who came to hear him speak of things of the spirit should not have to endure the discomfort of an empty stomach as they listened.

Jesus made it clear that, since body and spirit must live together on this earth, the needs of both must be catered to with equal concern and, by implication, he sought to impress on woman that the value of the food she cooks is greater than mere feeding. In effect, Jesus was assuring her that unless the mortal body is sustained, the immortal spirit that dwells within it may remain beyond reach.

Undoubtedly, that evening at Cana, there must have been more than a few guests who had already had too much wine by the time Mary made her plea. In fact, these were the very persons who could have made trouble at the feast if more wine had been refused them. Must one assume that, by providing more wine, Jesus was condoning excessive drinking? If we know anything about his way of life and his teachings, we also know that the answer must be 'no'. Why, then, did he make further temptation possible? For one thing, trusting his mother's judgment as he obviously did, he assessed the general harm that might come to the assembled crowd from the unruly behavior of a few irate drunkards, against the advantage of keeping them quiet until they could be carried away without breaking up the feast. His decision also suggests that reasonable men should know how to resist temptation of their own free will. Of this he had already set a dramatic example by struggling against his own temptations in the wilderness. He was saying, as well, that 'things' are the servants of man who has the power and the ability to regulate their use if he will discipline himself to do so. Inevitably, the thought of self-discipline brings once again into focus a responsibility of woman, for it is in childhood that this essential tool is forged.

The Gospel relates that the steward of the feast was as surprised by the superlative quality of the wine as he was by its very appearance, having been told that none was available. In his view, at that stage of the festivities there was no need for excellence. But Jesus was a perfectionist and, once he had decided to provide the wine, it would not only be superlative, but it would also be abundant. When he said to the servants, "Fill the jars with water," he intended that the "six stone jars standing near" each with a twenty-gallon capacity, all be filled—and they were. For woman, whose plea he answered in such generous fashion, the lesson is: if an act is worth performing, perform it to the full and when you give, give unstintingly and of your best.

The very nature of wine itself, contains a special message for woman to consider. Wine, as everyone knows, is the natural juice of grapes transformed by its inner process of fermentation into a more sophisticated and powerful beverage which, from time immemorial, has had an honored place in religious ritual as in secular celebrations. Symbolically, the natural juice may be likened to the gifts with which a human being is endowed at birth and the wine to these same gifts after they have been transformed and sublimated by the ferment that occurs when the human mind grows and matures. Man, however, has taught himself to develop ideal conditions for the production of great wines and so should the best conditions be created for the development of human talents. But, just as heady wine must be taken with restraint, so must highly developed talents be judiciously put to use.

Thus, a dual role for woman emerges from the symbolism implied in the nature of the wine. First, like the grower tending his vineyards, who prepares the soil and keeps it nourished, she too should prepare and feed the mind in which a child's talents begin to grow, that they be neither stunted nor go prematurely to seed. Next, like the winemaker who keeps an eye on fermentation, she must watch the young mind in ferment, helping a process in which talents are neither abused nor ignored.

The ministry which began at Cana lasted three years and it is only at its very end that wine reappears in the Gospel narrative with prime significance. As at Cana, so at the Last Supper in Jerusalem, the meal marked a celebration: the wedding feast was gay, noisy and secular; the Seder for the feast of the Passover was solemn and religious, a simple ritual meal shared by twelve men in an atmosphere in which love struggled against suspicion and fear. At Cana the wine bespoke a beginning, in Jerusalem a tragic conclusion.

Although woman was absent from the table laid that last evening in an upper room on Mount Zion, she was made present, nonetheless, by the symbolic significance introduced by Jesus as he blessed the bread and the wine. At Cana Jesus had identified wine with a woman, his mother; in Jerusalem he identified it with his own blood. Woman and blood are carriers of life: she nurturing life within herself, blood making life pulsate through the body. By identifying wine with blood Jesus inevitably identified wine with woman through their common and equally indispensable relationship to life. At the last supper, he blessed the bread and the wine calling them his own body and blood and, having shared them with his disciples, bade his eleven faithful repeat the ritual in memory of him. As the centuries raced on, leaving changes in their wake, this was to remain the great Christian act of 'outreach', gathering all manner of people—women equally with men—into communion with God and among themselves. On that last evening in Jerusalem, the significance of the wine had fully revealed itself. The ministry that had begun with the changing of water into wine to celebrate a covenant between man and woman who were in no way equal had come to an end with the changing of wine into blood to celebrate a covenant between God and humanity that assures the perfect equality of man and woman in the promise of redemption.

4

The Hem of His Garment

As soon as the boat bringing Jesus across the Sea of Galilee was sighted from shore, a multitude rushed to the landing ready to hear him speak. But Jesus had scarcely set foot aground when the president of the synagogue, a man called Jairus, thrust his way through the crowd and, kneeling before him, implored the Nazarene to come to see his twelve-year old daughter who lay at the point of death. Jesus went with him at once and the crowd followed them, shoving and pushing not to lose the Master who was moving briskly in the lead.

A pale, sickly woman who hugged her clothes about her as if she were cold despite the sunshine, had joined the multitude at the shore. But she had not come to hear Jesus speak: all she wanted was to get close enough to him to touch his garment when he passed. For twelve years, the best of her life, she had been afflicted by a loss of blood and not one of the many remedies she had tried had even improved her condition. All her substance had been spent on physicians and their medicines and now, having grown weaker and worse through the years, she was also destitute. One day she heard that a prophet had come into Galilee whom John the Baptist had called the Messiah and soon afterwards she had come across acquaintances who had seen him gather crowds all over the countryside. They said that the Galilean did not scold or threaten hellfire and brimstone when he spoke, as did John. He was kind in manner and gentle with words and wherever he went a glow seemed to envelop those around him. Someone told her that the love in his eyes kindled a fire in the souls of those who looked into them; another said it was the way in which he used familiar facts to explain his new and exciting promises that held the people spell-bound; others, again, believed that he was indeed the Messiah and this, the woman felt, would explain everything that happened around him. One person had assured her that he could perform miraculous deeds, such as changing water into wine which, this person claimed, had occurred at Cana in Galilee during a wedding feast.

The sick woman had listened to all these accounts, turning them over in her mind and finally a new wave of hope suddenly stirred within her. Indeed, more than hope, it was the inexplicable certainty that if she could only touch the garment of this extraordinary man, she would be healed. She did not want to hear him speak, much less speak to him, and she knew that, according to Mosaic law, she was ritually unclean and anyone or anything she touched would become unclean also. She risked severe punishment if anyone in the crowd discovered that while she suffered from a flow of blood, whether natural or due to illness, she had allowed herself to touch a man, or had been touched by him. Therefore she had to pass unnoticed, brush his garment unseen and not let anyone find out what her ailment had been once she was healed.

Struggling to inch her way through the crowd, stumbling on the rough stones as she went on, she stooped not so much from fatigue or the need to be inconspicuous, as from the profound wave of humility that had come over her as soon as she had laid eyes on Jesus when he landed from the boat. Moreover, if she remained bent, as she was trying to remain, once she reached the top of the motley procession and was directly behind the Galilean, she would be in the perfect posture to touch the hem of his robe. Dusty as the hem would be, with the dust of many roads, it would convey his healing power—of this she had not the slightest doubt.

Finally, her face dripping with sweat, she was within reach of her goal. She quickened her step, not to lose an inch of the ground she had so painfully gained, stretched out her arm and hand, her knees so bent she seemed about to fall to the ground and, suddenly, the tips of her fingers brushed the hem of the Galilean's robe as it swung out from his feet. Perhaps it was as though sparks were racing through her body, setting her afire. Perhaps the flash lasted only one extraordinary moment followed by a sense of coolness as from a mountain breeze. Perhaps, a long-forgotten buoyancy suddenly pervaded her being, giving her the certainty that she had been cured.

She may have been too overwhelmed to utter a cry when the sound of a voice brought her back to reality. Someone was saying: "Who touched my clothes?" and another voice answered: "You see the crowd pressing upon you and you ask who touched you?" and the first voice rejoining: "But someone did touch me, for I felt that power had gone out from me." The woman raised her head and her eyes met the eyes of Jesus, his face leaning towards her with tenderness. Falling to her knees she blurted out her story and Jesus, as if he wished the crowd to understand why the miracle had occurred, said loudly enough for all to hear: "Daughter, your faith has healed you. Go in peace, forever free from this trouble."

Not only had Jesus healed the woman, but he had, once more, publicly assailed the wickedness of a law devised by men to keep woman in subjection as a creature of scarce account. Deliberately, Jesus made it impossible for her to conceal the nature of her ailment or to deny that she had touched him, so that all, including the president of the synagogue, would have proof before their very eyes, that he had no use for a law that considered a woman "unclean" in her circumstances. By rewarding her with a miracle for touching him, he showed his defiance of the law as well. It was one more deed wrought by him that day to affirm the equality of woman in legal and in ritual terms.

As suddenly as Jesus had stopped, leaned down and spoken to the crouching woman, he turned away and briskly resumed his walk alongside the anguished father whose little girl needed his help. The woman who, having sought anonimity had become the center of attraction because Jesus had healed her, was now alone on the dusty road, a changed and healthy person. But of one thing only was she conscious as she started homeward: the words of the man of Galilee were swelling up in her heart with a magnificent crescendo: "Go in peace, your faith had healed you."

Impossible as it may be to establish a precise chronology of the events which occurred as Jesus began his ministry, in the Gospel narrative the public healing of the humble and silent woman comes as the first of its kind. To be sure, Jesus must have performed earlier healings, otherwise why would Jairus have come to plead for his daughter's recovery, but this is the first that Jesus himself made public, even as it is the first time that the Nazarene's words, "Your faith has healed you," appear in the record.

The essence and core of his entire doctrine is contained in this overpowering statement, for the salvation he offered to all humans was to be achieved by the individual's own faith and volition.

That day, to the sick woman and to the crowd, he was saying that she had been cured by her own faith, a force she had nurtured within herself strongly enough to draw power from him. "I felt that power had gone out from me" Jesus told his disciples, signifying that it was not he who had used his power to heal her, but she who had taken it from him to heal herself. Since a woman was the object of his words, the implication of them must be that, now as then, any woman capable of making such faith grow within herself has power to compel a greater power than her own to act for her sake. Jesus, be it noted, did not qualify the woman's faith, by calling it 'your faith in God', or 'your faith in me' or, even, 'your faith in yourself'. The very simplicity of his statement asserts that faith is one, flowing into many different channels.

More than once in the Gospels we find Jesus reprimanding those around him, including his disciples, for their lack of faith— "O ye of little faith" were the words he used and always without further qualification. As he embarked upon his ministry, the Nazarene found his people caught in a decline of the faith that had sustained them through the centuries. Their faith in God, in morality, in their fellow man and even in their own destiny was vacillating. This, Jesus evidently believed, could lead to a collapse of the nation of Israel, even as the sins of faithlessness committed in the Temple would reduce the Temple of Jerusalem to rubble.

A similar lack or decline of faith has become characteristic of today's world. The more technologically advanced the society, the sharper appears the decline of its faith so that science and its derivatives are being blamed for the condition, as though faith and science could not exist or grow together. It may well be woman's task in her partnership with man to dispel this untenable assumption. If faith is essentially the ability to accept as real something which does not fall within the purview of the senses, any scientifically proven fact testifies to the power of faith, since every forward step taken by science must be propelled by an abiding faith in a goal as yet unproven and still intangible. Every human discovery arises from an intuition which must be investigated and developed until it becomes transformed into fact. Hence the history of any scientific achievement is evidence of a faith impervious to the slings of failure and stoically persistent in its quest for proof. Although, in this context, faith is not intended to have a religious connotation, it is worthy of note that many of the world's great scientists, inventors and discoverers have seen no conflict between faith in God and faith in the scientific method.

Regardless of its particular nature, faith is a source of strength without which no human being can survive effectively. This includes the atheist and the cynic who, believing that they can live without faith in God or man or anything in between, obviously survive because of their faith in their ability to survive without faith. And this, too, of course is a form of faith.

The Nazarene's emphasis on the woman's faith rather than on his or on God's power to heal, contains two implications significant for all women: one, that faith is needed for the support of life, as the sick woman proved; the other, that faith is a form of individual power capable of attracting power from others as the power of the sick woman's faith attracted the healing power of Jesus. A further implication for woman to take to heart is that the Galilean, having found woman capable of such faith and having rewarded her unflinching use of it, even for as personal an objective as the restoration of her own health, was bidding her to help others to follow her example in understanding and using their own faith.

The sick woman possessed at least two other qualities, perhaps enlivened by her faith yet capable of independent growth. She was an optimist, uncowed by illness and destitution; she had sufficient will power to compel her weakened body to make the journey to the Sea of Galilee and to overcome the confusion and the pressure of the crowd packed between her and her goal. Probably also, thrown upon her own resources by her long malady, she had learnt to practice and to appreciate silence, withdrawal into herself and maybe meditation as well—these being less than common in women. But the Nazarene's praise of her faith implicitly praises these qualities as well, suggesting their importance to all women.

Interesting in this episode is the fact that, whereas nearly all the sick, the blind, the maimed, the mentally deranged and other sufferers, publicly and often loudly implored Jesus to heal them, the woman of Galilee made no such plea. Her silent striving to touch the healer's garment was her own form of prayer, but she never gave voice to it, convinced, as she seems to have been, that if Jesus had power to heal he would also have power to see what was in her innermost being. As Mary had done at Cana, stating the shortage of wine and asking for nothing, so the sick woman made her case by her mere presence, without pleading to be healed. The wordless prayer was immediately answered.

By virtue of her faith the woman knew that no material obstacle could impede the flow of spiritual power, therefore she sought only to touch the healer's robe, eager to remain unobserved. Jesus, instead, first by declaring that, without his knowledge, someone— the sick woman, obviously—had drawn power from him, and then by dismissing her "in peace and forever free from this trouble," was saying to her and to all women that to the humble of heart and the strong of faith, such a theft of power was rewarded with a gift of grace.

Maybe the first of the Nazarene's publicly performed healings involved a woman because he wished to highlight the fact that woman, in general, has a strong intuitive feeling for the supernatural. She is given to sensing its existence and believing in its workings, even if in so doing she may have to bypass reality or even common reason. By rewarding the woman's reliance on the supernatural, when all natural or human healing efforts had failed even vaguely to affect her condition, Jesus revealed the high value which he placed upon it. The implication of the reward is that woman must neither underestimate her tendency to sense and to experience the supernatural, nor ever misuse it.

What is most surprising about this particular episode is not that it involved a middle class woman of very average intelligence and education, for Jesus sought out this type of person in preference to the rich, the brilliant or the exalted. Rather, it is that, in a public situation in which a large majority of the crowd must have been average men who regarded woman as chattel, Jesus so deliberately drew attention to her soul by speaking of her faith. He knew how a predominantly male crowd would feel about the mere presence of women. If they came with him from elsewhere into a town or village, the women might be frowned upon, ignored or even ostracized, and tolerated only because of Jesus. The younger men usually accepted the presence of women as persons, but the opposition came from older conservative men who continued to treat woman as an object. Perhaps, when Jesus kept Jairus and the crowd waiting while he reassured a woman for whom he had performed a miracle and sent her on her way with a blessing, he was merely emphasizing to Jairus and the other men that in the eyes of God as in his own, woman was their equal. Certainly on that dusty road in Galilee, Jesus showed his belief in the spiritual equality of man and woman, pointing to it as a fundamental element of the total partnership for which modern men and women must set their sights.

Like every change in society, like every forward step to be taken, accepting partnership as a way of life requires a considerable measure of faith by men as well as women—faith in each other, faith in their own contribution to the partnership, faith, be it religious or not, in the power of their spirit to strengthen their minds as well as their hands for the unprecedented challenge. The healing of the sick woman in Galilee is a clear demonstration to woman of how she shall do her part in using faith with persistence as well as humility.

5

The Living Water

In olden times, the traveler reaching Samaria from the south came upon a well, just outside the town of Shechem, locally referred to as the Well of Jacob. Slightly off the dusty crossroads, it was a good place to rest. The sun was already high over the valley when Jesus and his disciples came to the spot after negotiating hills and rugged passes on their way from Jerusalem to Galilee. There was a sense of coolness near the well where water, splashed and spilt by the women who came to draw from it, kept the stones moist, mitigating the heat of the air.

Jesus, wearied by the two-day journey, decided to wait there while the disciples went into the town to find provisions for the remainder of their trek. Despite the risk of attack by Jew-hating Samaritans, he had decided on the shorter route through the Samarian hills in order to cut two days from the five required to return to Galilee from Judaea without leaving Jewish soil. Jews and Samaritans came of one stock and worshiped the same God, but for several centuries the Jews had been treating the Samaritans as outcasts because the latter had failed to preserve the purity of the race.

The historical fact was that, seven hundred years before the time of Jesus, the Samaritans had been forced to intermarry with the Assyrians who had invaded and conquered their country. Because of this, the Jews had decreed that the Chosen People could have no further dealings with their neighbors, share food or drink with them, or allow them to worship in Jerusalem's temple. For seven centuries the Samaritans, had been smarting under this injustice and frequently took revenge by attacking Jews who traveled through their territory.

While Jesus waited at the well for the disciples, a woman came to draw water, paying no attention to him until he said: "Give me to drink." Realizing from his garments that he was a Jew, in astonishment she answered: "What! You a Jew ask drink of me a Samaritan woman?" Jesus, instead of giving her a direct answer, amazed her all the more by saying: "Woman, if you only knew what God gives and who it is that is asking for a drink, you would have asked him and he would have given you living water."

Unable to grasp the meaning of the stranger's words, the woman had become totally puzzled. "Sir," she asked, "you have no bucket and the well is deep: how can you give me living water?" The question had barely left her lips before her inborn distrust of Jews made her suspect his motives and, with severity in her voice, she added: "Are you a greater man than our ancestor Jacob who gave us the well and drank of it himself and his sons and his cattle?" Once more, the answer she received was not on the same plane as her question. Without refering to Jacob, Jesus told her: "Everybody who drinks this water will be thirsty again, but whoever drinks the water I shall give will not suffer thirst again. The water that I shall give, will be an inner spring always welling up for eternal life." Quite obviously, the woman sought down-to-earth replies, while Jesus strove to transport her thinking to a spiritual realm that was beyond her reach.

Water, for her, represented the daily necessity of bringing it up from the well in skins, pots or buckets and using it with parsimony. Persisting in her practical concern and hoping the stranger might indeed relieve her of the endless task, she rejoined: "Sir, give me that water, then I shall not be thirsty or have to come all the way to draw." Clearly their thinking was still traveling on very different tracks until Jesus, changing his approach, exclaimed:

"Go home, call your husband and come back." Now, awed by the stranger's tone that rang almost like a command, yet captivated by the man and unable to deceive him, she blurted out: "I have no husband" to which Jesus quickly added: "Yes, you are right in saying that you have no husband for, although you have had five husbands, the man with whom you are now living is not your husband. You told the truth there."

His knowledge of her private life startled her. "Sir" she murmured, "I can see that you are a prophet" then, at once recaptured by her initial suspicion of him who being a Jew could not be a friend, she challenged him abruptly saying: "Our fathers worshiped in this mountain, yet you Jews say that the temple where God must be worshiped is in Jerusalem." No doubt she reasoned to herself that if he was a prophet and a seer, he would be able to explain the exclusion of her people from the temple in Jerusalem. Moreover, since he was willing to defy Jewish laws by asking her for water and offering to give her his in return, he might also be ready to ignore the Jewish tabu against men talking to women about God. Jesus did not evade the challenge. "Believe me," he answered, "the time is coming when you will worship the Father neither on this mountain nor in Jerusalem. You Samaritans worship without knowing what you worship, but the time approaches, indeed is already here, when all who are worshippers will worship the Father in spirit and in truth. God is spirit and those who worship him must worship him in spirit and in truth."

Had the woman finally understood? In that one stupendous phrase, Jesus had proclaimed the equality of all who are believers in God, an equality not of body, mind or estate, but of the spirit which dwells in every person. He had proclaimed an equality fulfilled in truth, because truth exists, recognized or not, heeded or not, in the deep recesses of every soul where, consciously or not, mortality is in perennial confrontation with the eternal.

Thus, sitting alongside a well in the quiet countryside of Samaria, an alien land, Jesus was laying down a great verity, not to his disciples or to learned men, but to a very simple Samaritan woman who was living in sin. Why? Merely to touch or redeem one woman who was not even of his own people? No, not merely to reach one woman but to speak to all women, however exalted or humble, rich or poor, bright or dull of mind, virtuous or sinful, women of that day or of any day.

Then Jesus fell silent, and the words he had spoken began to take on their true significance in the woman's mind. As though a ray of unexpected light had penetrated her obtuseness making her understand the nature of what he was saying, she told him: "I know that Messiah is coming, and when he comes he will tell us everything." Presently, from the Nazarene's lips, with dramatic simplicity, came the revelation: "I am he. I, who am speaking to you now." Never before had he been willing to answer the question, 'Who are you?' so frequently asked of him by friends and foes alike. It was a woman who had not asked it, who received the fateful answer: he was the Messiah.

The Samaritan looked at him in silence and, for a brief moment, time appeared to stand still, absorbing the sound of his words. A translucent sky, a valley basking in the sun, a backdrop of hills stately in their robes of light and shadow, had become witness to the unique encounter between a prophet sent of God and a simple woman who, in her namelessness, represented all womankind. Sinful as she was, suspicious as she had been and overly concerned with trivial matters, unable at first to comprehend what she had heard, the Samaritan was suddenly awake to a new and startling reality.

The scene is easy to envision: the woman, holding her skins filled with water, cool with the coolness of the rock from which it had sprung, and leaning against the well, motionless as though lost in a dream. Jesus, not far from her, standing silently as though listening to the murmur of the leaves and to the breathing of myriad creatures animating the earth and air about him. The sudden and unexpected revelation of his mission had been as a stone cast into the pool of human hope, creating rings that would widen and widen generation after generation, age after age, forever renewing the impact of the stone's first thrust.

When the disciples returned to join Jesus at the well, the

Samaritan woman was still near him, but none of the men dared
ask: 'What do you want?' or 'Why are you talking with her?' No
doubt the wave of grace that radiated from him to envelop the
woman, also reached into their hearts and sealed their lips. The
barriers of prejudice that Jesus and the woman had reduced to
shatters, seemed present only like the broken pieces of some object
now despised and useless. Presently, as though responding to an
impulse, the Samaritan picked up her water skins and went off in
the direction of Shechem, walking at a lively pace. She was going
to fetch the men. At the edge of town she began to call out:
"Come and see a man who told me everything I ever did. Could
this be the Messiah?" They came out of the town following her to
the well where they saw the Galilean, spoke to him and believed.
The Gospel says: "Many Samaritans of that town came to believe
in him because of the woman's testimony . . . they pressed him to
stay with them; and he stayed there two days."

Strangely enough, the Gospel narrative contains no word about
what Jesus said or did in the two days with the 'outcast' people of
Samaria, a striking contrast to the careful record of his dialogue
with the woman at the well. The spotlight of the Gospel is on her,
revealing the respective faults and virtues that Jesus had seen
in the laxity of her morals and in the spontaneity of her truthful
answers, in her persistent emphasis on temporalities and in her
sudden concern with God and how to worship Him, in her
suspicion of the stranger because he was a Jew and in her eagerness to tell her people that he was the Messiah.

Out in the open countryside, by the edge of a well into which
mountain springs fed water for human sustenance, was the place
from which Jesus chose to take flight as preacher of the Word.
Here he delivered his first known sermon, a brief and luminous
definition of two strong pillars on which his teaching was to stand:
"God is spirit" and 'I am the Messiah." He chose alien soil,
through which a Jew would travel at some risk, a spot made
majestic by nature's hand, a temple whose walls were mountains
and whose cover was the sky. Not in an enclosure set aside for
worship, from which man, by his own self-serving will, excluded

those he deemed unworthy of entering its precincts, but in the open countryside, next to an ancient well, was where it all began.

The first convert, the first person to know Jesus as Messiah and to suddenly comprehend the nature of God's being—'spirit'—the first to be sent to convey the message to others, was a foreigner, one treated as an outcast by the Nazarene's own people, a creature of scanty morals and scantier intellect and, most unthinkable of all, a woman! Thus, even as at Cana, for the sake of a woman, Jesus embarked upon his ministry to people, signifying service, so at Jacob's Well, in touching a woman's soul, he initiated his mission to souls, signifying redemption.

Although the Gospels give the Samaritan no name, nor describe her physical features, the story of her encounter with Jesus at the well makes possible the reconstruction of her personality. Having had five husbands and now living with another man, she was probably nearing forty; not well-to-do, because women of means used to send a servant to fetch water from the well; not shy, for when the stranger spoke to her she answered without hesitation. She took pride in her people and resented the Jews who, by tradition, had become their enemies. She had a strong enough intuition to feel assured that the stranger meant no harm and, in her soul, a faith that made her expect the coming of the Messiah. But even as we imagine her thus in our own mind, it is her actual facelessness and anonimity that so importantly transform her into a symbol of all womankind. She, the unsophisticated recipient of vital spiritual revelations, is sent to convey them to the men who, accepting her amazing testimony, like her, also became 'believers'. Her part as messenger to men of mystical truths which, beyond her ken at first, are suddenly comprehended, is only one aspect of her vaster role as the equal partner of man. The role's other facets emerge from the implications of her encounter with the Nazarene and from the words he speaks to her. Their meaning for the woman of today is clear.

First, and without preamble, addressing the woman with a brief and unequivocal request, 'Give me to drink', Jesus breached the seven hundred-year-old wall of prejudice and racial arrogance that the Jews had built to isolate Samaria. Then, just as rapidly as the dialogue began between Jesus and the woman, so did the wall disintegrate and finally collapse. Alas, history proves that the victory won at Jacob's well against prejudice was scarcely more than a token, humanity being afflicted and undermined by its evil influence to this day. Nonetheless, the principle had been established, the lesson taught by word and deed.

Since Jesus chose a woman to share his attack on this evil and be his partner in defeating it that day, the implication seems obvious that he deemed her to be a major force in the battle that would have to be fought continuously against it. The fact that his attack on prejudice was couched in a request for water underscores his choice of woman rather than man as the person best suited to take on the struggle—water, the element indispensable to life being indissolubly linked with woman who, from time immemorial, has drawn it from its source and carried it to all living things. There is more. Racial prejudice is predicated upon the accident of birth and women, sharing as they do the universal sameness of the experience of giving birth, must instinctively perceive the evil absurdity of this prejudice and be willing to destroy it.

Second, Jesus offered the Samaritan 'living water' for thirsting souls in return for a drink of water for his thirsting body. After which, as if it were the normal thing to do, he bade her call her husband, implying that she should share the spiritual gift with man. But she, hoping only that the stranger's offer would liberate her forever from the servitude of the well, did not understand what he really meant. Only after Jesus, casting light into the depths of her conscience, lifted up the burden of sins that weighed upon her entire being, did her mind begin to comprehend his language. Here, once more as on other occasions when his masterly touch was revealed, Jesus demonstrated to her and to posterity how to deal with the human psyche. He was a superb psychologist.

What the modern world takes credit for discovering or, at least, developing into a science or discipline, Jesus was putting into practice two thousand years ago. Time and time again, and usually in connection with a woman as though to show her how to use her talents in this field, Jesus did for love of people what is now too often poorly done by so-called professionals, who have more love for what their subject can pay than for what the person is. Jesus knew that the sense of guilt preying on the woman's conscience blocked his access to her heart and mind. His sudden command to the Samaritan, "Go home, call your husband and come back," apparently unrelated to what he had said before, was the most effective of shock therapies. Taken by surprise, she blurted out, "I have no husband," and the lid of secrecy was loosened. Then, without waiting for her to add what Jesus knew would have to be her admission of sinful conduct, he spelled out the nature of her burden, without comment other than to note her truthfulness: "Yes, you are right in saying that you have no husband for, although you have had five husbands, the man with whom you are now living is not your husband. You told the truth there."

Jesus did not qualify her way of her life or reprimand her for it, since his purpose was now achieved. Her mind, relieved and made responsive by the stranger's respect for her feelings as well as by his extraordinary insight, was now open to a flow of new ideas. In fact it was she and not Jesus who immediately raised the dialogue to a higher plane. Although her allusion to injustices done to her people by the Jews sounded like a challenge, her question to him was about where to worship God. There was balm in the stupenduous answer she received: "God is spirit . . . the time is coming when you will worship the Father neither on this mountain nor in Jerusalem . . ."

Jesus knew so well how to touch the chords which make the spirit come alive that he all but instantly transformed a simple woman, suspicious of him and far less concerned with saving her soul than with saving time on her physical chores, into an inflamed missionary who could scarcely wait to share her spiritual treasure with the men of her town.

The astonishing dialogue conveys its message to posterity as much by its implications as by its words. But whereas the words, written into the record, speak to men and women alike, their implications are intended for woman whose presence at the well endowed them with their unique significance. First, Jesus was trying to make the Samaritan and every woman recognize her essential role in trying to reach the inner person as he had reached her. Therefore she must strive to understand human psychology and anticipate its reactions, recognizing the conditions and circumstances that bring them on. Next, by making her break down an absurd yet rooted prejudice, he was implying that woman was best equipped to take this kind of action because she tends to become more deeply involved than the average man in the human and social concerns of those around her.

When to her gift of intuition woman adds her efforts to understand the mind of her fellowhumans, men as well as women, changing their lives as Jesus changed hers, her contribution to her partnership with man becomes incalculably enhanced. One woman's determination to eliminate prejudice by persuasion, if multiplied by the similar determination of her peers, is capable of altering the climate of an entire community. In fact, this is probably what the Samaritan woman did, when she ran off to communicate to others what she had learned from Jesus and brought them to him that they might learn more. She changed the climate of her community.

However, once we recognize that the scene at the well is replete with implications for all womankind, another question inevitably comes to mind, begging an answer: why did Jesus choose this unsophisticated woman to be the recipient of the momentous revelation that he was the Messiah? There can be no doubt that she was chosen deliberately for this role, since the decision to make the revelation could only have been his own or commanded by the Lord. Why did the Galilean tell her, who appeared to be so completely earthbound in her thinking, about worshiping God "in spirit and in truth", or that the time had already come "when you will worship the Father neither on this mountain nor in Jerusalem"? These were statements without precedent in his teaching and their significance tremendous: by these words, Jesus was making a direct attack on the religious structure supporting the self-serving power of a priesthood that claimed to have exclusive, divinely-granted control over man's access to his God. The Samaritan was the least likely person to perceive the full reach of his charge against the priests and, even less, to know how to react to it.

It is precisely because the Galilean's choice appears to be so unlikely by average human standards—and, of course, his ministry was directed to ordinary mortals—that one feels compelled to try to analyze its purpose in simple human terms. Clearly, his new and indeed revolutionary definition of how to worship the Father carried the timeless and universal significance inherent in all his teaching. While it delivered a blow to an exalted body of powerful men, it was designed to serve the needs of even the simplest people seeking God, by eliminating the barrier erected by the priests between the Father and His children. "God is spirit" he said, "and those who worship him must worship in spirit and in truth." All human beings are endowed with a spirit and every spirit is capable of seeking truth, in however simple terms he may perceive it. It was the true link between humanity and God that Jesus re-established by those words.

It must be remembered that many Jews thought it likely that woman had no soul, and that Jewish law regarded Samaritans as inferiors and outcasts. In addressing himself to a woman, neither very bright nor very virtuous and a foreigner besides, Jesus was speaking these truths to a person who in his time and society would have been considered unworthy of hearing them and incapable of understanding them. If Jesus could make the Samaritan comprehend his message, he could feel certain that almost anybody else would understand it.

Having demonstrated his belief in the fact that woman like man was endowed with a soul, Jesus selected a woman whose mind and spirit appeared deaf to any call but that of temporal desires and needs. Her soul, when he first approached her, did indeed seem non-existent. By relieving her conscience he brought her soul to life. The change was swift and overwhelming, for she could scarcely wait to share her new exaltation with those who had not yet experienced the indescribable inner transformation.

The Samaritan must have been known to the people of Shechem for what she was, especially to the men, five of whom having married her had also divorced her, a prerogative of the husband which the wife was powerless to contest. She was, at that very moment, living in sin. Yet Jesus chose her to convey his startling spiritual revelations to her townsmen who, at once, believed her testimony. This must certainly signify and, in fact, prove, that a spirit redeemed radiates an irresistible power, sufficient to instantly overcome distrust of the allegedly soulless female, and to wipe out the justifiable contempt in which she must have been held for her reprehensible conduct.

In essence, the Nazarene's decision to engage in a dialogue of such far-reaching significance with a woman tells the woman of today that she too, like the Samaritan, can be redeemed without seeking redemption and can become bearer to a male-governed society of revelations as spiritual or as revolutionary as those which Jesus chose to make to the water-carrier two thousand years ago.

6

The Guilt of the Accusers

The Jewish feast of the Tabernacles was in its last day. Jesus, who at first had decided not to participate, had instead arrived in Jerusalem in the middle of the celebration and gone into the temple to teach. As usual, a large crowd immediately gathered around him and his popularity so irritated his enemies, chiefly scribes and Pharisees, that they ordered the temple police to try to catch him committing some infraction of the law. The police, instead, attracted by his magnetism, drank in his words and, like the majority of the crowd, soon felt convinced that the Rabbi from Nazareth was indeed the Messiah.

At dawn of the next day Jesus was again in the temple, helping an ever larger crowd to understand the Scriptures. Again several of his enemies were there, hoping to trap him. Some were scribes, penmen or copyists as their title indicates, who, having mastered every part of Scripture, also taught it. Others were Pharisees, an exclusive sect of zealous teachers of Mosaic Law, who also watched rigidly over its interpretation. Jesus criticized them for being more legalistic than charitable and for making a public display of their piety.

Suddenly, while Jesus was speaking to a crowd that listened spellbound, several scribes and Pharisees rushed into the temple, pushing a woman they had caught in adultery. Shoving her in front of Jesus, one of them said to him in a loud tone of voice: "Master, this woman was caught in the very act of adultery. In the law Moses had laid down that such women are to be stoned. What do you say about it?" Knowing the human compassion by which Jesus was so frequently motivated—a virtue they feared as well as despised—they hoped he would yield to it in behalf of the woman and thus be caught defying the law.

As with other women who briefly hold the spotlight in the Gospel, the adulteress is given no name, nor is anything said about her except that she was facing death for breaking the seventh commandment. Probably young and attractive, she must have been terrified as she stood alone before the teacher's seat, surrounded by smug males out for blood in which to drown their spite. The temple must have been ringing with their shouts, when the self-righteous Pharisee imposed silence enough to voice his question, but the place remained filled with suspended anger, likely to erupt against the Nazarene if his answer displeased them.

Their victim probably looked at Jesus pleadingly, but he merely bent over and began to write on the ground with his finger, apparently as oblivious to her as to the crowd or to the fact that an answer was expected of him. As he continued to move his finger, writing, the mood in the temple changed from anger to curiosity. The men pressed closer to the teaching seat, trying to peer over each other's shoulders to find out what the Rabbi was doing. Although the Gospel record does not say so, we may well guess that some voice may have been raised asking: "Master, what are you writing?" or that someone from the back may have echoed it saying: "What is he doing? Why doesn't somebody tell us what he is doing?" The woman, still encircled by her accusers, though afraid, seemed forgotten. The men's curiosity increased, as they looked around with puzzled expressions, their fingers still clutching the stones.

As unexpectedly as Jesus had begun to write, so did he sit up, declaring: "That one of you who is without sin shall throw the first stone", then "once again he bent down and wrote on the ground." Since he was never hasty, his tone was certainly calm and the words spoken with a deliberateness that conveyed finality as though, having stated the obvious, no comment was required.

No man dared be the first to throw. As soon as the eldest among them walked out of the temple, the others followed, hastening to drop their stones outside the holy precinct. The space in the temple where they had stood was now empty save for Jesus and the woman, who, although free, still seemed unable to move. The Galilean did not raise his head or stop writing until he sensed that the accusers had gone, then he looked at her, simply asking: "Where are they? Has no one condemned you?"

Death had just passed her by and the terror of its nearness must still have been upon her as she looked at the Rabbi who had saved her life and, barely raising her voice, murmured: "No, sir." Aware of her guilt, since she had been caught in the act, she must have expected him to reprimand her or perhaps to impose some kind of penance for her wrongdoing. But Jesus merely smiled adding: "No more do I. You may go; do not sin again." When she walked out of the temple into the sunshine, her whole being flooded by a sense of relief mixed with a strangely indescribable joy, she cannot have known what the teacher who saved her life had done for womankind.

That morning in Jerusalem's temple, with a few simple words, Jesus had overturned another vitiated interpretation of a commandment of God—thou shalt not commit adultery—and dealt a blow to another time-honored tradition of injustice to woman. Quietly and firmly he had made it clear that the burden of sin falls equally on man and woman. Mosaic law in fact decreed that both should be stoned if caught in adultery but, almost without exception, the male was allowed to escape. That morning the situation had been no different, no male having been brought into the temple with the guilty woman. And the erudite men who came before Jesus to demand justice certainly knew full well that they were breaking God's law.

What made their conscience respond so quickly to the Galilean's firm injunction that they walked away, sparing the woman's life? Had they never before heard the voice of conscience or, having

heard it, had they always arrogantly refused to heed it? Or, per- *conscience*
haps, was it the Rabbi's unique way of penetrating the very depths
of the human soul that had forced them to recognize their sins?
This certainly must have been the first time that such self-satisfied
and highly-placed men had had their guilt revealed in public and
must also have been the last thing they expected to have happen
to them. The man from Galilee, now a redoubtable presence in
Judaea as well, had to be stopped. They had placed a fateful decision in his hands, knowing that if he supported their interpretation of Mosaic Law and the adulteress were stoned, forever after
they could ignore their own conscience if it ever rumbled loud
enough to be heard. They could also forget the absurdly protective
position that the carpenter was always taking in favor of women,
and have no qualms about treating her as chattel which their laws
declared her to be. But Jesus had decided otherwise.

Eluding the trap that had been set for him, he placed the accusers and the accused on the same ethical and moral plane, wiping out in one stroke the mere idea that privilege can be allowed
to prevail over the law. In fact, the Pharisees and their cohorts
were claiming a double privilege in demanding the adulteress' life.
They were claiming it as males and as protectors of the law itself.
Dragging the woman before the crowd as a sex object, they had
degraded her even beneath her chattel status, but Jesus, in full
view of both those who believed in him and the accusers who
hated him, immediately treated her as a human person, no different
from the man. As such, if she were guilty her sin would be no
greater than that of the male caught with her, and, since their joint
act involved bodies made equally of flesh and blood, if the act
were sinful for one it was likewise sinful for the other. In a short
sentence, Jesus had erased the privilege to which the male had laid
his false claim for endless years.

Not only did Jesus' answer equate the guilt of man and woman
committing the same breach of the law, but his words carried a
broader implication as to the actual significance of sin. Since his
answer did not define it as adultery, the term applied to any and all
sin which any of the accusers might have on their conscience at

that moment. On this occasion, as always in his teaching, the Nazarene was blending the personal with the universal: nothing is more personal than the commission of a sin and the admission of it by the sinner's conscience, therefore he was addressing the individual conscience of each man; yet his use of the term sin expressed the entire spectrum of wilful error and embraced all of humankind. Nonetheless, he was also telling woman that the inferior status to which Jewish society had relegated her did not give her license to behave as an inferior being, since she was, in fact, a complete person endowed with a soul as well as a body and must, therefore, behave accordingly.

Once the accusers had departed and the woman's life was no longer endangered, Jesus quietly offered her forgiveness and redemption, two concepts she had probably never thought of, or certainly never thought of as applying to herself. Any judge, however compassionate, who might have forgiven her wrongdoing and warned her not to sin again as Jesus did, would almost certainly have added that if she broke the law once more, she would not escape punishment. He would have been trying to purchase her good behavior with a threat. Jesus, instead, placed her on her honor. "Go and do not sin again" was all he said, thereby paying a moving and splended tribute to her battered womanhood and to the spirit dwelling within her ill-used body. He appealed not to her understanding of the law, nor to her fear of retribution, but to her conscience and her heart.

To the simple men who were still in the temple hoping he would resume his teaching and who had seen the drama come to its unexpected conclusion, he was also making it clear that the dictates of conscience must be stronger than those of the manmade laws. To the adulteress whose life had been saved by virtue of this principle and to all others suffering, like her, from the burden of some sin, he was implicitly declaring that conscience, first of all, should thereafter guide their actions and their lives.

Primarily for the woman's sake, but for all mortals as well, when he began to write on the ground, Jesus offered another stupendous lesson—this time in sheer human psychology. The mood of the accusers, influential custodians of Mosaic Law, was one of impatience, scarcely able to wait to be proven right or to catch Jesus in a breach of the law. The mood of the men who followed them into the temple, ready to cast their stones at the adulteress, was one of aroused evil, sparked by the anticipation of being able to assert their superiority as males. The atmosphere in the temple was too highly charged for Jesus to defuse it with an immediate answer, unless, of course, his answer had been: "Stone her!" No matter what else he might have said, the stones would literally have flown out of those eager hands, using him as a target. Violent feelings confuse the mind and obfuscate judgment.

Conscious of these elementary facts, which few leaders seem to pay attention to when they are trying to communicate with a crowd, Jesus leaned down to write, as though he had not heard the question or the voices clamoring all around him. As the minutes passed—perhaps five, ten or more, we do not know—the voices began to subside. Impatience—'what are we waiting for?'—edged out anger, but wonder soon edged out impatience—'what is the Rabbi doing?'—changing the mood from rage to curiosity. When Jesus raised his head, looking at the accusers and speaking in a voice that was calm yet loud and clear, the men's minds, no longer prey to fury, understood what he meant. Nothing in the Gospel suggests that any Pharisee or scribe, or any man holding a stone, reacted vocally when the Rabbi said: "That one of you who is without sin shall throw the first stone." Greeted by stunned silence, his words must have echoed through the temple leaving their memory forever etched into the stones.

But Jesus also knew how human emotions operate and that the calming effect of his words had to be maintained until the woman was completely safe. Therefore, he leaned down again to write, as if resuming a task he had only briefly interrupted to answer the Pharisee's question and again now commanding his complete attention. The swiftness of it all must have left everyone gaping, especially those who had come to the temple to hear the Rabbi from Nazareth speak of love and who had almost witnessed a horrible display of hate. Perhaps, however, they learned more about love from the Nazarene's extraordinary disposition of the frightened woman's case than they would have from his explanation of the ancient Scriptures.

When Jesus sensed that the woman's accusers had departed, he raised his head, looked at her and immediately placed himself on her footing by asking her to tell him what had happened—"Have they gone? Did anyone condemn you?"—as though he were not aware of what had been occurring. When he dismissed her, she was sufficiently at ease to grasp the significance of absolution without penance, which was precisely what she had received while Jesus was saying to all womankind, 'A woman has just been rescued from death of the soul as well as death of the body. Did you see what I did? Did you hear what I said in order to save her? Use all this as guidance for yourselves'.

His imaginative device of writing on the ground to break up a vicious mass mood, was the demonstration of an instrument—a psychological instrument—with which to play upon the hearts and minds of all human beings. He had shown how to handle and overcome the power of violent emotions, how to transform spite into reason, vindictiveness into compassion, arrogance into forgiveness. Since all of this had come about because of a woman's near-fatal plight, the implications seem intended particularly for woman to perceive and to understand. Jesus was saying that if woman will but let her intuition guide her in sensing the feelings of those around her, guide her decision as to when and how to act, when and how to speak in others' behalf, she could be an inspired healer of hurts and frustrations, a smoother of the abrasiveness of modern life.

If the responsibility of understanding the twists and turns of the human psyche, as they occur in everyday life, is to be seen as one that Jesus would assign to woman, we must then view it as part of her mission of 'inreach'. On that morning in the temple when an isolated drama was being played out, Jesus revealed his own power of 'inreach' in the most masterly of ways. Everything he did and said was outwardly most simple, but its purpose was to reach into the conscience of each person involved, from the

Pharisee who asked Jesus the question to the woman whose life was at stake, touching scores of other men who witnessed the surprising outcome. It was a demonstration of the power of inreach and it did not entail a miracle or the use of supernatural faculties. It brought into play factors which ordinary mortals can lay claim to: a sense of justice, a knowledge of facts [Jesus knew Mosaic Law and saw how it was being circumvented], an understanding of human emotions. Jesus had merely shown how to bring these elements together and how to affect the human response. It was a universal lesson in human psychology, which in his strong and tender hands had become the instrument of rescue and redemption for a woman caught in sin.

7

A Doer, a Dreamer and the Restoration of Life

Bethany was a quiet village whose flat-roofed houses congregated around the shoulder of the Mount of Olives, forming a suburb of Jerusalem which was less than two miles away. Although its Aramaic name—Bethany—signified 'house of poverty', the population included several well-to-do families. For instance, Martha, Mary and their brother Lazarus, Jesus' dearest friends, were people of means who gave generously of their substance as well as of themselves. Jesus occasionally stayed with them for a few days at a time and frequently brought his disciples there to dine, joining other guests who, like them, dropped in at meal time.

Martha, the eldest and probably widowed, was an open-handed and efficient homemaker, whereas Mary, who appears to have remained single, was a dreamer and a mystic. Regardless of these differences, however, the sisters were very close to each other and they loved Jesus with total devotion. He, in turn reciprocated their love, enjoyed their company and evidently considered them his most intimate friends. His disciples were also his friends, of course, but in a different way: Jesus was grooming them to inherit his mission and his ministry. The two women, instead, were as sisters to him.

One day he found Martha more involved than usual in household chores and somewhat out of patience with Mary who, as soon as Jesus came into the house, sat at his feet, her face glowing with anticipation of his words. After a while, Martha, increasingly harassed, appealed to Jesus saying: "Master, you do not care that my sister has left me to get on with the work by myself? Tell her to come and lend a hand." Her tone of voice no doubt suggested that she thought Mary was being lazy and shunning her duties in the house. Jesus, far from disturbed by Mary's failure to devote herself to such activities, quietly replied: "Martha, Martha, you are fretting and fussing about so many things, but only one thing is necessary. The part that Mary has chosen is best and it shall not be taken from her."

Behind these two short sentences lay far greater meaning than was expressed by the words. Jesus was pointing out a scale of values and establishing an order of priorities. As sometimes happens to all of us, Martha too, that day, seemed to be making the meal more important than the guest, the means more significant than the end. Mary, instead, was forgetting the means and the meal in preference for the end which was to be near Jesus, not losing a moment of his presence or a word that passed his lips. Martha's "fretting and fussing about so many things" ran counter to the Nazarene's predilection for simplifying the business of daily living to the uttermost. Mary, instead, had chosen "one thing" which was for the spirit, as against the "many" that were for the flesh.

Who among us, like Martha, has not sometimes behaved as if things intended for the use of people, were more important than people? This transposition of values, that could occur even in the simple life-style of Martha's day, has become an overwhelming condition in the life-style of our time. We rate ourselves and others according to the "things" we have or how much "status" they provide, rather than on the basis of how few "things" we need and how little they are able to control our mind and spirit.

Actually, in Jesus' society women had no choice between giving precedence to the activity of the mind or of their hands. The latter came first. The former, implying a woman's quest for intellectual improvement was frowned upon, made difficult to achieve, if not altogether forbidden. The friendly reprimand to Martha in support of Mary's engrossment in whatever stimulated her mind and spirit, was one more of many lances that Jesus was constantly breaking for the rights of woman. He believed in the equality of male and female intellects, and therefore in the right of men and women to develop, and cater to, the needs of their minds as they did to those of their bodies—indeed, more so. The human mind is as much a gift of God as human hands and woman has not been shortchanged in her share of it. But a repressive and anti-feminist society, such as the one to which Jesus himself belonged by reason of his birth, believed that woman should work her hands to the bone but allow her intellect to lie fallow. In fact, most men honestly believed that women had no such thing as 'intellect' in their make-up.

Long past were the times when a woman of Israel could rise to the height of political power, as did Deborah, more than eleven hundred years before the birth of Jesus. As a young woman, she combined homemaking with letting neighbors and outsiders discuss their problems with her. The word spread that, having an overpowering faith in God, she also had the gift of knowing how to instill it in others. Patriotic and brave, as well as faithful and wise, she had taught herself all she could about the Canaanites, who were then the oppressive rulers of the people of Israel. Angered by the lack of courage and leadership she saw in the men who should have led an uprising against their oppressors, she rose publicly to denounce their apathy and to prod the masses into action. Taking it upon herself to call a capable general out of his retirement, she helped him organize a military operation even as she convinced him that faith in the Lord would serve him better than the weapons his soldiers lacked. Barak, the general, agreed to take the people of Israel into battle only if Deborah was at his side. "If thou wilt go with me" he said, "then I will go; but if thou wilt not go with me then I will not go." Deborah went with him, spurring the troops with her courage and faith. Since then, how many millions of men have said to a woman: 'I would not attempt this were you not here to help and sustain me'? They are uncounted, of course, and yet the indispensable necessity of establishing this partnership of men and women as a basic factor in governing human society is only just beginning to be perceived.

Later, under the reign of King Josiah, there was Huldah, recognized as a prophetess throughout Judaea, and also as a woman whose wisdom was spiritual and whose knowledge was scholarly. The temple of Jerusalem had undergone extensive repairs under that King, and in the course of them a long-lost Book of the Law had been unearthed. Differences of opinion arose among priests and scholars as to the authenticity of the scroll and it was to Huldah that the King deferred the final judgment on the matter. She is believed to have taught in a temple school, her home across from the temple area. That she was an expert of renown is certain, otherwise why would the King have sent such a precious document to her house, carried by five of his messengers including the high priest? That her authentication of the scroll was accepted without question is demonstrated by the fact that, no sooner had the messengers returned it to the King, than he put into action the Laws written within it and now found in the Book of Deuteronomy. The two temple gates were named "Huldah" in her honor.

Esther, a humble Jewish orphan, raised in captivity in Persia, became queen of that land, not merely because of her beauty but also, and perhaps chiefly, because a cousin, Mordecai, had given her a superior education. King Ahasuerus had seated her with him on the throne of his empire, not knowing that she was a Jewess. Haman, her husband's favorite, had planned the extermination of thousands of Jews and Esther made the perilous decision of going before the King, a step not permitted her by law, to plead for her threatened people. After fasting and praying, using the common sense and self-control that had won her the love of Ahasuerus, and saying, as the Bible records, "So I will go in unto the King, which is not according to the law and if I perish, I perish," she appeared before him and won protection for the Jews. The history of any people tells of women who, combining their intelligence with their power of 'inreach', caused men to change their course of action.

Yet, to this day, other women admire them as unique figures, instead of regarding what they did as a challenge to themselves in making better use of their own intellect and inner powers.

When Jesus was in Bethany some four hundred years had elapsed since Esther's time and the condition of the Hebrew woman had suffered a sharp decline, as Jesus' struggle to correct it shows. That day in Martha and Mary's house, when he supported the younger sister's right to set aside her chores and indulge the demands of her inquiring mind, Jesus was trying to restore what he regarded as woman's birthright. He was insisting that woman's role was not exclusively, or even primarily, that of the homemaker —that if woman chose the intellectual life she had "chosen the better part." In standing by Mary he was inviting uncounted millions of women, through the ages, to discover the wonders of their own mind and thus find release from the dreariness of the material tasks from which they could see no escape. He was urging the Marthas who were at heart potential Marys, to teach themselves how to put their intellectual capacity—whatever its scope—to its fullest use. In essence, what Jesus was really saying was that the 'doer' could also be the 'dreamer'. He saw the will to do and the will to dream not as forces in conflict, tearing the person apart in a contest for supremacy, but as equally important elements of the complete being, each balancing the other in fulfilling the demands of the mind as fully as those of the body.

In reality, Martha, who has become the prototype of the woman 'doer', was herself a woman of great faith and of active intelligence. What may have annoyed Jesus that day was that, having a good mind, she "fretted and fussed" so much about household things. Necessary as they were, he wanted her to take them in her stride, do them as a matter of course but without allowing them to enslave her or to deprive her of the joy and riches of 'dreaming'. However, when Jesus said that Mary 'had chosen the better part' only "one thing" being "necessary" he can hardly have meant that by chosing the intellect woman would have to exclude all other activities and concerns. Certainly he must have meant that having chosen what was "necessary", such a choice should have precedence—remembering that whatever affected mind and spirit was more important than what affected body and matter. However, though Martha was bustling around the kitchen more than Mary, she was fully aware of the power emanating from the mere presence of Jesus in their house. She was as convinced as her sister that nothing was impossible for him and her faith was soon put to the test.

One day, when Jesus was teaching on the banks of the river Jordan, surrounded as always by eager followers, a messenger from Bethany sought him out. Sent by Martha he brought Jesus the sad news that Lazarus "your friend, lies gravely ill", and the tone of his voice revealed urgency as well as concern. Surprisingly, Jesus showed no inclination to rush over to Bethany, but only replied: "This sickness will not end in death; it has come for the glory of God, to bring glory to the son of God." Much as he loved Lazarus and his sisters, he made no move for two days, to the relief of the disciples who knew that Judaea was no place in which Jesus should make an appearance at that time. On his last visit to Jerusalem his life had been threatened.

When he did finally say to them, 'Let us go back to Judaea' they tried to dissuade him: "It is not long since the Jews were wanting to stone you. Are you going there again?" Jesus replied: "Our friend Lazarus has fallen asleep, but I shall go and wake him." One disciple immediately rejoined: "Master, if he has fallen asleep, he will recover." But Jesus had used the word 'sleep' to signify death and therefore felt obliged to make his meaning clear. "Lazarus is dead" he said. "I am glad not to have been there; it will be for your good and for the good of your faith. Let us go to him." Thomas, who later was to doubt the Master's resurrection, turning to the others added bravely: "Let us also go, that we may die with him." They all went to Bethany and no harm befell Jesus or those who accompanied him. On the road all sorts of people had joined them and, apparently, it was quite a crowd that arrived at the sisters' house. But they were still some distance from Bethany, when Martha was seen running towards them in a state of grief and agitation.

When she came within earshot of Jesus, her voice breaking, she cried out: "If you had been here, sir, my brother would not have died. But even now I know that whatever you ask of God, God will grant you." Standing still she heard him give her an answer that did not satisfy her: "Your brother will rise again." Though still upset, she was able to rejoin: "I know that he will rise again at the resurrection on the last day." No doubt she lacked courage enough to add that she wanted Lazarus alive on earth, right then, but Jesus knowing what was in her mind added: "I am the resurrection and the life. If a man has faith in me, even though he has died, he shall come to life; and no one who is alive and has faith shall ever die. Do you believe this?" "Lord, I do," she answered.

Once again, as when he spoke to the Samaritan woman at Jacob's Well, it was a woman who drew from him the declaration of what was to become an article of faith for all Christians: "I am the resurrection and the life." Martha, like the Samaritan, failing at first to understand, was then suddenly convinced. Her declaration of faith had no sooner left her lips than she ran back home to find Mary. "The Master is here," she said, "and asking for you." At once, Mary rushed out of the house, following Martha to the place where Jesus still tarried.

The dramatic events that ensued cannot be told better than in the words of John, the Evangelist, who recorded them as follows: "So Mary came to the place where Jesus was. As soon as she caught sight of him she fell at his feet and said, "O sir, if you had only been here my brother would not have died." When Jesus saw her weeping and the Jews her companions weeping, he sighed heavily and was deeply moved. "Where have you laid him?" he asked. They replied, "Come and see, sir." Jesus wept. The Jews said, "Could not this man, who opened the blind man's eyes, have done something to keep Lazarus from dying?"

"Jesus again sighed deeply, then he went over to the tomb. It was a cave, with a stone placed against it. Jesus said, "Take away the stone." Martha, the dead man's sister, said to him, "Sir, by now there will be a stench; he has been there four days." Jesus said, "Did I not tell you that if you have faith, you will see the glory of God?" So they removed the stone.

"Then Jesus looked upward and said, "Father, I thank thee: thou hast heard me. I knew already that thou hearest me, but I spoke for the sake of the people standing round, that they might believe that thou didst send me." Then he raised his voice in a great cry: "Lazarus, come forth!" The dead man came out, his hands and feet swathed in linen bands, his face wrapped in a cloth. Jesus said, "Loose him; let him go."

This was the last of his great miracles before his death. True, during his final visit to Jerusalem, for Passover, when the blind, the maimed and the sick surrounded him in the streets begging for mercy, he healed many of them, but he did not know any of them individually and the healings were unplanned. The case of Lazarus was different. Moved by the grief and the entreaties of Martha and Mary, Jesus went to Bethany intending to use his powers to bring him back to life. It must have been clear to him that the women felt certain that he could release their brother from death.

The raising of Lazarus marked the conclusion of Jesus' ministry of human service—the mission to bodies, so to speak, that began with the miracle at Cana—and one cannot fail to note how both the supernatural events that initiated and closed the cycle had been his answer to the pleas of women. There seems to be no indication that Mary, his mother, knew Martha and Mary of Bethany, yet the similarities that link them can hardly be ignored. They did not appeal to Jesus for themselves: at Cana, Mary wanted the groom's good name to remain unscathed, at Bethany Martha and Mary wanted their brother's life to be restored to him. They all had faith in the willingness as well as in the power of Jesus to grant their request and they did not lose faith when his response was delayed. They would derive no personal profit from his action. Mary obviously had no use for some two hundred gallons of wine and the household of Martha and Mary would not be financially affected by the absence of Lazarus. Each woman, however, was inwardly seeking a benefit from the miracle for which she had pleaded, albeit a benefit without negotiable value: Mary wanted assurance that her nephew would not lose his good name and Martha and Mary had faith that life could overcome death. These were the intangibles which Jesus valued most highly—the replacement of anxious concern with relief and of sorrow with joy—and of these the women received a full share.

The resurrection at Bethany, we learn from the Gospels, was one of three such acts wrought by Jesus, in addition to his own. And it is significant to find that all four were closely linked to a woman. One, and according to some, the first, was the bringing back to life of a twelve year old girl; the other two were young men, Lazarus and the son of the widow of Nain, whose lives he restored because he was moved by the grief of the women who loved them. The first evidence of his own resurrection he chose to reveal to a woman. Did all this occur by coincidence? Was anything ever a 'coincidence' in his ministry? The very accounts of his life and the whole purpose of his mission among mortals show that the answer is no. Indeed, from every record we have that dates back to his time, what emerges most clearly is a pattern in which the minutest detail has its own indispensable place. Was the pattern preordained or predestined, constituting a track from which Jesus could neither escape nor depart? Or, instead, was the pattern the fruit of his own insight and foresight, a self-imposed course charted by a spirit and mind fully aware of the ultimate goal? To these questions there never has been and there never may be an answer beyond refutation. The best that our finite yet speculative minds can attempt is to study the pattern we see, and evaluate every particle of it. From such a process the inreaching role of the woman, whose factual part is well told in the Gospels, emerges with a significance that cannot be ignored, even though it is more often implicit than clearly spelled out.

The repeated association of a woman with the overcoming of death seems to be saying that she, whose body can bring forth a new life, is also endowed with a spirit, whose love and faith deserve to be rewarded with the miracle of resurrection. Not only is Jesus making woman aware of her spiritual power, but he is resorting to the highest demonstration of his own supernatural power to impress upon a male-governed society the irrefutable fact that woman, far from being the 'object' man would condemn her to be, is a person with a soul equal to his.

The first life he restored belonged to a very young girl, the daughter of Jairus, a Jew of high standing and the elected ruler of his synagogue. She was approaching death when her father rushed to find Jesus on the shores of Lake Galilee. He came to implore the Rabbi from Nazareth to prevent her from dying. The faith in *Jairus* his heart must have glowed through the tears in his eyes as he stood by the edge of the water, beseeching the extraordinary preacher to make haste and come to his succor. Quickly agreeing to go to Jairus' house, Jesus was walking at a brisk pace, followed as always by a vast crowd, when he suddenly stopped. Everyone seemed surprised but, as we view it in retrospect, the reason for the halt is clear.

With Jairus as witness, Jesus intended to violate a rabbinical law that affronted the dignity of woman. Thus, turning to his disciples he asked, in a peremptory tone, who in that multitude *issue of blood* had touched his garment. He must certainly have known who, by 'drawing power' from him, had been healed at that moment. But, at the cost of embarassing the sick woman he had cured, he caused her to make public her condition as well as her recovery, leaving no room for doubt that, by law, she had made him unclean. He gave her his blessing and sent her on her way, satisfied that everyone present had not only seen his violation when he acknowledged that she had touched him, but had also seen it sanctioned by the silence of Jairus. Indeed, the Jewish leader may not have been the only man in the crowd who came to realize that Jesus valued the dignity of woman more highly than he did a decree which only served the ego of man.

Just as this strange interlude ended, a messenger from Jairus' house ran up to his master saying: "Your daughter is dead. Do not trouble the Rabbi any further." Jesus, overhearing the message, reassured Jairus saying: "Do not be afraid. Only have faith." Then, taking with him only Peter, James and John, he rapidly followed the grieving father to his home. If the child was only in a coma, as some critics have suggested, nobody in Jairus' household knew or believed this to be so for, when Jesus arrived, the funeral rites had already begun. Allowing only the girl's parents and his three disciples to enter the room in which the child lay, Jesus tenderly took her hand in his, raised it and said: *Talitha, cum*—'Maiden, get up.' At once the girl opened her eyes, got up and walked. Aware as he always was of human needs, Jesus told the child's mother to quickly give her food, after which he instructed those present not to reveal to anyone what had occurred. But, as he probably foresaw, word spread like wildfire reporting his miracle and, his enemies added, his violation of ritual laws as well.

Indeed, no less than three times in that one day had the Nazarene publicly broken a rabbinical decree: he had allowed an 'unclean' woman to touch him, immediately thereafter he had entered Jairus' house without performing the ritual purification and there, he had taken the hand of a corpse into his own. What must have galled his enemies above all was that Jairus, a high ranking religious Jew, had accepted the miraculous gift of his child's return to life from the Nazarene's hands, not even remotely indicating an awareness that anything less pure than God's grace might have touched them.

The two other persons Jesus raised from the dead were men whose bodies he did not touch and whose lives he restored to quell the grief of women who loved them. One of these, a widow he encountered on a road near the village of Nain, was weeping disconsolately as she followed the bier of her son, her only child and only support. Halting the funeral procession, Jesus said to her: "Weep no more" and she, startled by the light in his face and by his daring to speak to her on the street, immediately stopped sobbing. Then Jesus laid his hand on the bier, loudly commanding: "Young man, rise up!" And the young man obeyed him as promptly as had the daughter of Jairus and as Lazarus would, not long after, when he walked out of his tomb.

Martha, too, was weeping when she rushed up to Jesus on the road outside Bethany, and to her also Jesus spoke. "Your brother will rise again," he said and, like the widow, Martha stopped sobbing. Suddenly calmed, both women were made subconsciously ready to withstand the shock of the miracle to come. The Nazarene's unfailing way with human emotions had been at work: his unexpected words had cracked the despair that gripped the minds of both women, making way for joy to stream in and sweep away their grief. However, once again and for the sake of women, Jesus had felt impelled to violate another time-honored decree: it was improper for any man, and disreputable for a Rabbi, to speak to any woman in the street or in any public place. "One is not so much as to greet a woman . . ." said the ancient text. Such a prohibition, making no distinction between harlots or other purveyors of lust on the one hand and all others including the man's own wife, daughter or sister, on the other, was an insult to all Jewish women and Jesus overlooked no opportunity to defy it.

What lesson, what mission or what role shall woman perceive for herself in these particular happenings? For one, the Nazarene's open and deliberate violation of arrogant codes and unjust rules, illustrates his belief that obstacles such as these, standing in the way of higher and rightful goals, must be removed. As we know, his society was divided mainly by sex barriers, designed to safeguard the superiority of the male, but modern society has its own barriers of arrogance and injustice which range far beyond sex. They separate and classify humanity by color and race, by social status and economic bracket, by degree of success and popularity ratings, by being 'in' and being 'out'. What Jesus did for woman and against the sex barrier, woman should do for all persons and against all barriers.

Dismayingly enough, many women whose lives have a limited horizon, or whose minds and interests do not incite them to break out of the mold of their own special group, seem to stand in awe of these barriers. When these limitations merely affect their own personality or their individual freedom, the problem—if they perceive it as such—is one for them to solve as they wish. But most restrictive rules and tabus militate against vast segments of society and must be eliminated. Public action may finally prove necessary to achieve this end, but the motivation for change must first come from the inner conviction of every concerned individual. The power released by personal example, when multiplied by the number of those who follow it, becomes irresistible. The woman who knows when and how to set an example can also set off a motivating force of overwhelming proportions. More often than not, what she lacks is self-confidence.

As the Gospels reveal, it was the personal example of Jesus, speaking deliberately to women wherever he encountered them, that gradually compelled his male followers to welcome woman in their midst and treat her as one of their own. The Gospels, the Letters and Acts of the Apostles and other contemporary records show that the recognition of woman as a person and her participation in the work and risks of the early Christian communities became typical of the latter's way of life. Their practice of equality proved more influential than if they had deliberately made a public display of disregarding anti-feminist mores and laws. However, the position of the Christian woman began to decline when, early on, the Church whose leadership was centralized under a single head, took on an ever-expanding role as a secular power, deeply involved in the political affairs of the western world. Very soon the Roman church reverted to the exclusiveness of the Hebrew priesthood.

Public protest against woman's continuing disabilities in the church as in many other fields, unquestionably has its part. But, now as in the time of Jesus, the influence of a group or of the mass is only as strong as the personal convictions manifested by individual action. Today, as it was two thousand years ago, a measure of personal courage is needed in daring to fall out of step, to break loose from the protective shields of prejudice, to thwart or reject conventions which, although they demean the decency of human relations, are accepted by the socially insecure who need the prop of snob-appeal. This is an area in which the influence of the woman who is equally without prejudice at the grocery store and at the cocktail party produces longer range results than she may imagine.

Another lesson for the woman of our time emerges from the capacity of Jesus to be moved by compassion, to condone human foibles, to make no mystery of his feelings and to show sorrow with tears. In singling out those passages of the Gospels in which Jesus' feelings come into play, it becomes immediately clear that they were never beyond his inner control. From anger, as he chases the vendors out of the temples, to tears of pity shed over the fate of Jerusalem; from tenderness in talking to children, to severity in chastising the lawyers; from love for a truly repentant sinner, to contempt for a hypocrite saying prayers where they are most likely to be heard by the priests; from grief to mirth, he knew, experienced and revealed the gamut of human emotions.

Today the notion is becoming increasingly prevalent that feelings must not be displayed, that an impassive mask is a sign of true character and that the analyst's couch is the only resort to cure emotional stress or prevent a breakdown. The reality is that inner serenity is the mainspring of emotional control, the spiritual mechanism which knows when to tighten and when and how far to release the manifestation of feelings. Like all the mechanisms governing our body and mind, this too takes shape as the whole person takes shape, growing from infancy to adulthood. And once again here, as in countless other ways, it is the mother more than any other influence who has the power to create the conditions in which every child is able to develop the serenity and the mechanism as best he knows how. If she seeks counsel for this challenging task from books propounding methods and theories she may well find confusion instead of reasonable advice. Methods and theories swing like a pendulum, from insisting on the strictest of disciplines to the total absence of any restraint, so that neither mother nor child may ever be able to discover the path to serenity, or achieve a personal sense of measure. To strive to imitate Jesus in his use and control of human emotions is to strive for perfection. Yet, for those who believe in his teaching, there are goals to be seen in his practice that lie well within the reach of ordinary human beings.

8

Two Coins Given, One Coin Lost

The Outer Court of Jerusalem's Temple, also known as the Women's Court, where, as a child, Jesus had been reprimanded by his mother, was a place in which, as an adult, he sometimes tarried, observing the crowd. A lover of nature and of the open spaces, the Nazarene felt constrained by the temple walls, but he knew that this stronghold of conservatism and opposition to reform was where he must fight for his beliefs, ready to die for them if he failed to win.

It was here that Jesus saw some of hypocrisy's ugliest manifestations. Combined with the arrogance of the priests, they turned him against an outwardly magnificent shell harboring ungodliness. Although part of the temple area, the Court of Gentiles open even to heathens usually looked more like a circus than a place whose ultimate purpose was to worship Jehovah, the one God. During feasts people from every corner of the Roman Empire could be seen there in their colorful costumes and their extraordinary headdresses. From black turbans to brightly colored veils flowing around the hair and shoulders of the women and covering the faces of some, the shapes and hues were innumerable. The Jews who came ostensibly to pray were easily singled out by the *taliss* worn so as to appear below their tunics. This white veil was ornamented with long fringes knotted three times to denote the thrice holy name of the Lord Yahweh. The court had become a bank for the money-changers who stood at their desks exchanging moneys they styled 'unclean', such as Greek or Roman coins, for Jewish pieces to be given to the temple as the price for salvation. Doves and sheep were sold there, as well as oil and flour, wine and incense used in the rituals, but most astonishing of all was the presence of cattle pushing through the crowd.

Early in his ministry, caught in this appalling commercialism, Jesus was seized with anger. Taking off his *taliss* he knotted the fringes together and began to whip the changers upsetting their desks and scattering their coins all over the marble floor. Scandalized by the unrighteousness, he had created a righteous scandal of his own not readily forgotten. Already on the first of his visits to Jerusalem, a disciple who knew the city well and took pride in the Temple, its greatest landmark, had pointed admiringly to the majesty of the walls, the glitter of the votive offerings, the richness of the marbles and inlays. But Jesus, addressing him and other people within earshot, had responded by declaring, in a tone that conveyed finality: "There shall not be left one stone upon another." The disciples may or may not have grasped the meaning of his prophecy, but they came to realize that their master's negative moments were usually brought on by Jerusalem, a city in which Jesus could see little good and found little to praise except the forbearance of the poor and the sick huddling pathetically all around.

Tuesday of the Passover week that was destined to bring his life to an end, found Jesus sitting in the Women's Court, close to the alms boxes. These thirteen containers, equal and shaped like a *shofar*—a ram's horn—were marked for separate purposes, such as bird-dues, wood, frankincense, gold for the mercy-seat, or *shekels,* the chief silver coin of the Jews, and six for freewill offerings. Appearing to be lost in thought, Jesus was observing the almsgivers. Some made their offering with ostentation after assuring themselves that the box they chose and the size of their coins were being widely noticed, while others, dropping their contributions inconspicuously and with reverence, went quietly on their way.

A woman, wearing a shabby widow's garment, pulled out two tiny coins from her pocket and, with a happy look on her emaciated face, let them fall into a freewill box. Jesus saw that her coins were the smallest circulated in the land. Called *lepta* in Greek and *perutah* in Hebrew, two of them were needed to make up the twelfth part of one *denarius* which, in turn, was the Roman coin of lowest value. The *perutah,* a bronze piece minted by the Roman governors of Judaea for the use of the Hebrews, did not show the head of Caesar in deference to the Jewish proscription of human images, but displayed the imperial title encircling a *simpulum,* the ladle used by the Jews to pour water for ritual purification.

Jesus, who had made no comment up to that moment, called the disciples to his side and said: "I tell you this: this poor widow has given more than any of the others; for those others who have given had more than enough; but she with less than enough has given all she had to live on." Irked by the scribes, Pharisees and others who displayed their superior estate as they moved conspicuously about in ornate garments, he had also said to his intimates: "Beware of the lawyers who love to walk up and down in long robes, and have a great liking for respectful greetings in the street, for the chief seats in our synagogues and for places of honor at feasts. These are the men who eat the property of widows, while they say long prayers for appearance's sake; and they will receive the severest sentences."

One must assume that some impecunious males must also have dropped small coins into the boxes, but Jesus chose to call attention only to the widow's gift. No doubt this was because the lot of a poor widow was usually worse than that of a poor man, and also because the inferior status of woman and the urgent necessity to improve it were his constant concern. But, more important than these reasons, his intention was to make his disciples and other men aware of the remarkable generosity and sincere religious faith inherent in the woman's gesture, since women were not obliged to go to the temple or to make an offering. Of her own free will she had given all she had, and her act had meant more to Jesus than anything he had seen happen in the temple. For him, the value of a gift was never in its material worth, but in the spirit prompting it, and the greatest motivation of all was love.

But if Jesus was focusing on the destitute widow in teaching his disciples a lesson he was also holding her up as an example to other women to take to heart and follow. Was he suggesting, by this, that women is capable of more selflessness and more generosity than man? Probably not, but rather that her practice of unselfishness can move others whose altruism needs prodding to make it prevail over many a self-serving pressure.

The widow's case was likewise admirably suited as an illustration of the relativeness of human values as well as of all other 'things' on this earth where nothing is an absolute: neither good nor evil, neither time nor space, neither hope nor despair, neither love nor hate, but only the spirit transcending the bonds of matter. If woman's mission, as Jesus saw it—her role in the partnership with man—was to be one of 'inreach', her understanding of relativeness would have to be one of her essential tools. Therefore he so clearly explained why the value of the widow's offering was greater than that of the rich: they had more than enough, she did not have enough, they were giving of the superfluous, she was giving of the indispensable.

Over the centuries a great deal has been made of Jesus' condemnation of the rich and of their possessions, based largely on one of his harshest sayings: "It is easier for a camel to go through the eye of a needle than for a rich man to enter the kingdom of heaven." In reality, he condemned possessions as such far less than the use man made of them or the pride he took in them. Again, it was a matter of the relationship of things to values, to conditions, to objectives. Later that same day, while revealing the extraordinary sophistication of his mind in dealing with a trap laid for him by certain of his enemies, he gave another crystal-clear illustration of the proper use of wealth and another example of how to 'relate' the elements of a case before arriving at a judgment.

The trap was laid in a question asked with a great display of pious zeal by certain Herodians, a clan of pro-Roman politicians, and certain Pharisees. One of them said: "Master, we know that you teach in all honesty the way of life that God requires. Are we or are we not permitted to pay taxes to the Roman Emperor?" The question was well calculated. If Jesus answered yes the crowd around him, hating the tribute going to Rome, would have disapproved of him; if he answered no, he would have been reported to the Roman authorities. But he said "Show me the tribute money", which meant that they would have to bring him a silver piece minted in Rome. Then he asked: "Whose is this image and inscription?" "Caesar's" they replied. Then Jesus said: "Render to Caesar what is due to Caesar, and render to God what is due to God." It was disconcertingly simple, and obviously Jesus saw nothing wrong with owning silver coins and having to return them to Caesar. On other occasions he made it clear that "where a man has been given much, much will be expected of him" and 'the more a man has had entrusted to him, the more he will be required to repay."

Apparently Jesus also felt that a lost coin was well worth the effort of trying to find it, for he made such an instance memorable as the subject of a parable with a highly spiritual meaning. Jesus told this parable in the presence of several Pharisees and doctors of the law who had been "grumbling among themselves" because "this fellow welcomes sinners and eats with them." He said: "If a woman has ten pieces of silver and loses one of them, does she not light a lamp, sweep out the house, and look in every corner till she has found it? And when she has, she calls her friends and neighbors together and says, 'Rejoice with me! I have found the piece that I lost.' " Then Jesus emphasized the point of the parable in these words: "In the same way, I tell you, there is joy among the angels of God over one sinner who repents."

In addition to stressing the importance of a repentant sinner, several interesting implications are found in this parable. For one, by describing the woman's normal efforts to find the lost coin, Jesus is giving recognition to the value and the use of money, otherwise not even indirectly would he have praised the woman for trying to recover it. In those days, and still to this day in some parts of the world, the housewife carried the coins of account in her headdress, almost like a crown or a tiara. Since they represented part or all of the family wealth, the woman was likely to be in serious trouble if her husband discovered that she had lost one. Therefore it was important that she look for it with the utmost diligence, also a fact which Jesus indirectly praised by recounting it. For another thing, if the parable conveys a particular message to woman it is that she must guard with great care the treasure entrusted to her as well as her own. And this must be taken to signify not only tangible treasure as coins of silver or gold, but treasures far more valuable because they are of the spirit and the mind.

It can certainly be said that the tenderness of Jesus gravitated towards the poor and that the rich were often the object of his strongest criticism. Nevertheless, he never intended or attempted to set the poor against the rich or one social class against another. His teaching applied to a higher world—a world of thought—in which ultimately such material distinctions become unimportant. He was equally at home with a prosperous Zaccheus or Nicodemus, as with a beggar, with whom he sat by the wayside. He did not regard wealth or prosperity as a form of sin but as a danger to be guarded against. It was not Jesus, but Paul who wrote: "the love of money is the root of all evil" thus bearing out the Master's belief that the peril was not riches but how you used them. What Paul is saying is not that money is the root of evil, but the love of it is. If to love money causes one to become subjected to its power, then money becomes a master and man cannot serve two masters, God and Mammon. All of which merely signifies that 'things' which constitute wealth are not evil or wrong in themselves, but they become so once they cease to be man's tools, or in fact his slaves obeying his command as he puts them to a decent and fitting use. It is interesting to remember that when Jesus was born, it was not the poverty of his parents that caused him to see the light of day in a miserable stable, but the fact that the inns were crowded. There is nothing in the record to suggest that Joseph could not have paid for a room at the inn, modest as the inn must have been. It was a set of circumstances in the life into which Jesus was about to be born that associated his birth with poverty. Later, as an adult engaged in his mission, poverty was his choice so that "he did not have a place in which to lay his head." At the start, however, the new-born child was also the recipient of gifts which came almost simultaneously from the highest and the lowest in the land. The shepherds brought him a lamb, the Kings brought him gold, frankincense and myrrh, symbols of luxury and wealth. All were accepted equally in his behalf and recorded for all time in the Gospels. Disparate as were the givers, their hearts were pure and this was what made the gifts equally acceptable.

Obviously neither in the widow's gift at the temple, nor in the parable of the lost coin is there any wealth involved, except in symbol. Yet, these two symbolic cases, so closely tied to woman, and so fully spelled out in the Gospels, must be intended to convey a particular message to women. In fact it is reasonable to assume that Jesus was using them to say to women that if money, or riches in any other form was theirs to give, they should give it unselfishly and with a joyful heart; if it were in their custody, they must spare no pains to keep it intact. In either case, the amount was of no moment. The woman who accepts this implied instruction from the Nazarene, cannot fail to understand that to follow it is not enough: that communicating it by virtue of her own example is more important.

A Catholic scholar, Leonard Swidler, analyzing Jesus' efforts to equalize the condition of woman and to raise man's respect for her, views this parable as the high point of his efforts. He writes that Jesus, while telling "three parables in a row depicting God's concern for that which was lost", in this parable "projected God in the image of woman. The first story was of the shepherd who left the ninety-nine sheep to seek the one that was lost; the shepherd is God. In the third parable, of the prodigal son, the father is God. The second story is of the woman who sought the lost coin, and the woman is God! Jesus did not shrink from the notion of God as feminine." In fact Dr. Swidler adds, "it would appear that Jesus included this womanly image of God quite deliberately at this point for the scribes and Pharisees [for whose benefit he recited these three parables] were among those who most of all denigrated women."

Regardless of how this particular interpretation may be viewed, the conclusion is inescapable that, by telling these three parables together to illustrate a common meaning, Jesus intentionally equalized the importance of their male and female protagonists. The shepherd finding his lost sheep, the woman finding her silver coin, the father finding his wayward son, all equally symbolize the quest and the recovery of a soul lost in its transgressions. In turn, this signifies that woman like man has the capacity to find lost souls and bring them home, where the means of redemption await them.

All of this, Jesus was saying in a very direct and personal way to a gathering of suspicious and extremely conservative Jewish men, but he was also addressing himself to all womankind. For them, he was casting light on an aspect of woman's role in society —indeed a mission far more than an aspect—that she shares in complete equality with man. It is the redemptive mission to souls and one that Jesus assigned to them contemporaneously even as he chose to tell the Parables contemporaneously. It is a mission in which man and woman, overcoming the limitations of sex as of society, became a partnership of spirits, their powers made interchangeable as well as interdependent by the singleness of their transcendent purpose.

9

The Extravagant Gestures

It was the custom in the East to wash the feet of an honored guest and to anoint his head with perfumed oils as soon as he crossed the threshold. But Jesus, dining in Galilee at the house of a wealthy Pharisee named Simon, was treated otherwise, his host's invitation having probably been dictated more by curiosity than by admiration or respect. Like many other Pharisees, Simon was scornful of Jesus because of the strange company he was wont to keep, yet curious about the attraction he exercised on all sorts of people and about the source of his power. But, eager as he was to discover what the miracle working Rabbi was really like, he apparently could not bring himself to treat his guest of honor as tradition required. He did not wash his feet or anoint his head, nor did he welcome him with the traditional kiss of peace.

Jesus was already at dinner, reclining on the low couch, propped on his elbow, his feet against the wall as custom ruled, when a woman, rushing in from the street, fell to her knees at his side as tears streamed from her eyes. It was accepted practice that anyone could walk into an open house even if a meal were in progress, but Rabbinical rule frowned on the presence of women where men were eating, and this particular woman was the best known harlot in town! Gasps were heard when she began to pour myrrh, a very costly oil, upon the Nazarene's feet. Then a great silence fell upon the men as they watched the tender care with which she performed her deed. But Jesus knew what thoughts were circulating in their minds, behind lips closed in hostility.

Turning to Simon, he said: "Simon, I have something to say to you." "Master, say on," his host replied and everyone listened intently as Jesus continued: "Two men were in debt to a money-lender: one owed him five hundred silver pieces, the other fifty. As neither had anything to pay with, he let them both off. Now, which will love him more?" Simon answered: "I should think the one that was let off more." "You are right," said Jesus. Then, looking at the woman, but still addressing Simon, he added: "You see this woman? I came to your house; you provided no water for my feet, but this woman has made my feet wet with her tears and wiped them with her hair. You gave me no kiss, but she has been kissing my feet ever since she came in. You did not anoint my head with oil; but she has anointed my feet with myrrh. And so, I tell you, her great love proves that her many sins have been forgiven: where little has been forgiven, little love is shown." Then he said to her who, though still kneeling at his feet, was now looking at him with rapture in her eyes instead of tears, "Your sins are forgiven." The men began to whisper to each other 'Who is this man, that he can forgive sins?' but Jesus, pretending he had not heard them, leaned towards the woman to say to her even more forcefully despite the kindness in his voice: "Your faith has saved you; go in peace."

Who was she? An ordinary harlot who, having first hoped to find customers among the followers of the Nazarene, had instead been touched and transformed by the very sight of him? Or was she Mary of Magdala, from whose youthful body Jesus had chased out seven devils? At all events she cannot have been Mary of Bethany, a woman of reproachless conduct who, on a later occasion, when Jesus was dining with Simon the Leper, did exactly what the Galilean woman had done—anointed him with costly oils. After centuries of study, theologians and Bible scholars still do not agree about the woman's identity, but what matters more is the significance of what she did. Her gesture reveals the humility of one who is truly repentant, the anguished seeking of one who finally discovers a door open to salvation and, in the extravagant use of the precious unguent, the joy of uncalculated giving by one who is no longer looking for counterpart.

The contrast between this woman and Simon is unforgettable. He, the picture of self-satisfied respectability, is a man not quite brave enough to do fully and well what he set out to do—entertain the controversial Nazarene. She, in no way respectable but immensely generous, is one who, in her quest for remission, hides nothing and does not try to hold back her tears. For his half-hearted hospitality, Simon earns the telling of a brief tale with an inescapable moral: if you seek love, offer forgiveness; if you seek forgiveness, offer love; whereas the sinful woman earns total forgiveness as well as a gift of bliss. Here, as ever, we see the Nazarene's rewards meted out with a sophistication which, although habitual in him, is ever new and refreshing to those who witness it. We see his mind assessing every visible act and gesture as well as every secret motivation before passing judgment.

Since the person who rushed in to anoint him could as easily have been a man, the fact that she was a woman gave Jesus one more opportunity to cast light upon the faith and sensitivity he knew woman to possess. Even though he did not deliberately approach this Galilean as he did the Samaritan at the well, who was immortalized by her conversation with him, he immortalized the repentant harlot by explaining the significance of her gesture to his host. Now, in the retrospect of two thousand years, we see the explanation carrying its message to women as clearly as it did then to Simon.

The message says: by her love and generosity this woman taught the Pharisees a good deal they should have known already; she not only reminded them of the rules of hospitality they had chosen to ignore, but she also provided illustration of a truth they seemed to have forgotten, namely that love and forgiveness complement each other. Therefore, imitate the courage shown by this woman in acting as she did, for it is not enough to keep love and repentance locked within one's heart. They must emerge into the open, in order that repentance be fulfilled by remission and love rewarded by a like measure of love. Cultivate your own courage, that you may set it as an example before any person who, like Simon and his guests, is too self-satisfied to answer the summons of humility. Finally that evening when, as Luke informs us, Jesus turned to his anointer saying: "Your faith has saved you, go in peace," he had publicly asserted once again that woman is a person, neither chattel nor a mere sex object even if her profession made her such. His constant efforts to restore dignity to woman and to magnify her soul had found fertile ground in this surprising scene.

A similar scene occurred later in Bethany when another Simon, a leper Jesus had cured, invited him to dinner six days before the Passover. Martha served. Lazarus, whom Jesus had resurrected, sat among the guests. Suddenly Mary came in carrying a pound of pure nard, the most expensive of ointments. Like the woman of Galilee, she knelt at the feet of Jesus spreading them with the fragrant substance and wiping them with her long hair until the whole house was filled with exquisite perfume. John describes what happened next: "At this, Judas Iscariot, a disciple of his— the one who was to betray him—said, 'Why was this perfume not sold for thirty pounds and given to the poor?' He said this, not out of care for the poor, but because he was a thief; used to pilfer money put into the common purse, which was his charge. 'Leave her alone' said Jesus, 'let her keep it till the day when she prepares for my burial; for you have the poor among you always, but you will not always have me!' " Matthew and Mark also relate this event but with slight differences. They say that Mary poured the costly ointment on his head instead of his feet; Luke agrees with John. According to Mark it was "certain of those present who turned on Mary with fury", whereas Matthew reports that indignation came from the disciples, but neither of them mention Judas as does John. Matthew, Mark and John equally report the remarks of the Nazarene: that the poor would always be with them and that, by anointing him thus, Mary was 'beforehand' with preparing him for burial. However, while his recognition of prophetic foresight in Mary's gesture implicitly commends her for acting upon her presentiments, the inherent meaning of his comment about the poor remains uncertain.

Sociologists who see Jesus as a social reformer and Christians who take the injunction found in Acts, "it is more blessed to give than to receive", as a command to give to the poor have long been puzzled by words which seem to accept the poor as an inevitable fact of life. The interpretations of them are as varied as they are numerous. Certain of them consider the words to be an open reproach to a society which, doing little or nothing to eliminate the causes of poverty, would always find the poor a living presence. Others say that Jesus was praising Mary's gesture because she too believed that man does not live by bread alone. It is not only the needs of the physical body which must be met but those of the spirit and mind as well. For these, the food is hope, love, beauty made visible and the kind of sensitivity knowingly displayed by Mary.

In considering the significance of Mary's gesture before looking more deeply into Jesus' remark about the poor, one cannot eschew comparing it with the same gesture performed by the woman of Galilee. The difference in their motivations is striking. The harlot was a repentant sinner seeking redemption even as she administered a lesson in hospitality to the wealthy host of the banquet she had crashed. Her motive was psychologically self-serving no doubt, but not materially selfish. Her gesture immediately lifted her above the mundane to the plane of spiritual things where remission lay. Mary of Bethany, instead, was not in need of redemption: she was in search of nothing except the joy of giving. She loved the Nazarene and wished him to receive every mark of love and respect. While we can only guess if she was aware that her gesture predicted his approaching death, Jesus, with whom she dwelt in mystical communion, certainly knew of her prophetic gift.

In fact, the Jewish leaders at the dinner could have looked back into their history to find such women as Miriam, Deborah or Huldah, to name but three, whose precognitive powers had been immortalized in the Scriptures. There had also been Anna who had declared Jesus to be the Messiah when the child was first brought to the Temple forty days after his birth. Now, on the eve of his death, Jesus was telling them that Mary of Bethany, their neighbor, ranked among her prescient predecessors. In declaring that woman was as likely as man to be endowed with high spiritual powers, he was adding one more stone to the edifice of her equality.

The convivial atmosphere in which the dinner started must have become uneasy after Mary had emptied her jar of nard and broken it in final tribute to the guest of honor eliciting Judas Iscariot's sour remark: "Why was this perfume not sold for thirty pounds and given to the poor?" How many of the disciples present would have believed that Judas would soon collect thirty silver pieces for betraying their Master? For all her perceptivity, even Mary cannot have sensed what Judas was about to do, otherwise, mystic though she was and a lover of peace, she would have stopped at nothing to thwart his dastardly plot. It was Jesus who put him in his place.

Returning to the Nazarene's remark about the poor, one cannot fail to notice his varied reactions to those who aided them. For instance, Jesus publicly praised a man who gave one half of all he owned to the poor, but issued a warning to anyone making a public display of almsgiving. "When you give alms" he said, "do not sound a trumpet" and again "let not your left hand know what your right hand does." Although he was frequently approached by beggars, there is no evidence that he ever handed out a coin. He fed them and found them shelter, he cured their bodies and healed their souls, he talked with them, treating them as equals while the Jewish elite looked on with disdain, but he gave no alms. The fact that he carried no money is not the explanation. Judas Iscariot, treasurer of the little community having enough of it in his keeping to be able to steal with impunity, could have handed over to Jesus whatever he needed. Martha and Mary of Bethany, well-provided and generous, would have given Jesus anything he asked for. Actually, we know that Jesus did regard almsgiving as a virtue, but what made it such was the quality of the giver's stewardship. For a gift to have value in his eyes it had to be given with humility, grace, spontaneity and an intelligent understanding of its usefulness. These factors were undoubtedly present in the gift of costly ointments by Mary of Bethany and by the sinner of Galilee. Both women anointed him with humility, had generously given of their substance to purchase the unguents and there was a charitable purpose in their giving, even if poverty there lacked a visible form. But poverty was there invisibly and not of the flesh, for they were anointing a guest whose host had failed to fulfill his duties thereby revealing poverty of sensitivity and courage. The women came forth to fill these gaps disregarding the possible consequences of their act. In fact, Jesus had to rise to their defense to quell the indignant men whose pride they had hurt and, by his praise of their act, gave them a place in history. This may well be viewed as a message to woman that, while to succor those with evident needs is the duty of society as a whole, to be concerned with the secret poverty of mind and heart is more specifically her task.

On both occasions the accent underscores hospitality, a word signifying much more than merely receiving guests. It also means "the quality and disposition of receiving and treating guests and strangers in a warm, friendly and generous way." In every age and society hospitality has been, and still should be, the expression of honest regard between human beings. On the whole it is offered more frequently by choice than by compulsion and, although each society gives to this offering a form of its own, from the most primitive to the most sophisticated, unless the motivation is genuinely altruistic hospitality becomes spiritual treason.

In myriad ways woman is deeply involved in hospitality. What she does or fails to do in thought as well as action can often spell the difference between betraying the spirit of it or giving it the effulgence it deserves. Hospitality as Jesus understood it, involves more than providing mere material comfort or entertainment for the guest. It demands the host's knowledge and understanding of him or her, and of prevailing circumstances; it means sharing and giving without expecting a return. True hospitality is a manifestation of brotherhood extending far beyond the physical act of receiving a friend or a stranger. It means knowing how to open the doors of the mind to new or even displeasing ideas and listening to them with courtesy and respect. This 'hospitality of the intellect' is stupendously exemplified by the relationship between Jesus and the women of his day. By inviting them to join his following alongside the men, he clothed them in a gown of equality which they had never been allowed to don before and made them come alive to the reality that they were full-fledged human persons. A perfect host, Jesus tried to induce his male guests, reared to regard woman as chattel, to recognize the qualities and attributes of mind and soul that woman's presence brought into the community and to rate these contributions at their proper worth. He never failed to come to the defense of any man or woman who was demeaned or hurt while under the spiritual roof that sheltered whoever chose to follow him.

However, when a mountainside or the edge of a lake became the 'home' to which his mere presence served as invitation to a crowd, his sense of hospitality impelled him to consider the sheer physical needs of those who, having gathered in quest of food for their soul probably expected none from him for their body. On such occasions men and women were equal participants in the working of his miracles. They laid down what provisions they had brought and Jesus, multiplying them before their very eyes, linked them all in a stupendous communion of wonder and of gratitude. They had come at his bidding to nature's house without walls, roofed only by the skies, uncertain of what the fare might be. They departed restored in body and reborn in spirit, never to forget the words that were to echo for all time from the four corners of the earth.

Jesus, the carpenter of Nazareth, the rebel Rabbi, the violator of inequitable usages and rules, the perennial wanderer without fixed abode knowing that the entire creation was his house and all the creatures in it equal in God's sight, was the most individually considerate host and the most universal that humanity had ever seen.

What made his appeal equally irresistible to enlightened spirits and to sinners was his tearing down of any barrier that partitioned the human race. The tallest of these divided the race by gender and stood against woman. Jesus, the perfect host, courted risks as well as unpopularity in order to implement the first rule of hospitality—the equal treatment of all guests. He did this for the sake of woman and for the fundamental good of the society of his day and of all time. Can woman today do any less than perceive the lesson and strive to put it into practice?

10

Pilate's Wife

Friday's dawn had only faintly begun to color the skies over
Jerusalem but the winding streets of the Holy City were already
teeming with pilgrims. A few riding and most on foot, they had
come from every corner of the land to celebrate the seven day
feast of the Passover. Many had camped overnight on the city's
outskirts, eating their ritual meal of roasted unblemished lamb and
bitter herbs before retiring. The morrow would be Sabbath, the
day when everything came to a standstill except religious cere-
monies and the out-of-towners were hastening to the markets
within the city gates.

As daylight grew brighter, the people noisier and the traffic of
carts and animals more congested, the Roman police became pro-
portionately more conspicuous, for they were under strict orders to
protect the Jews from anything untoward during the High Holy
Days. Although this whole vast area was now the Roman province
of Judaea, the right of the Jews to observe their rituals and abide
by Mosaic Law was guaranteed by the Imperial Governor himself.

Pontius Pilate was holding that exalted post for the fourth year
and as on three previous Passovers, he and Claudia Procula, his
wife, had come from their official residence at Caesarea to be in
Jerusalem for the feast. The Jews were likely to get out of hand if
they were seized with a wave of religious fervor and it was well
for the Governor to be on call. Claudia knew that her husband

could barely wait for the affair to be over, but Pilate would have trembled had he known that the Friday upon which the sun was just rising was destined to be a day so fateful as to change the course of world events. A day which, with tragic irony, would also immortalize his name.

Long before dawn a strangely silent prisoner, apprehended in the night, had been brought for trial to the Fortress Antonia, a sullen place near the great Temple across town from Pilate's palace. Only a few people knew about that prisoner. They included the Roman Guard on duty at the fortress; the chief Priests, Captains and Elders of the Temple—powerful Jews who, having had the man captured, were already in the court of trial—a motley crowd of men without domicile or occupation who hung about any public place likely to provide them with a free show; and, remaining behind locked doors in various parts of the city, several men and women who had been followers of the prisoner, too afraid to move.

The prisoner was a carpenter from Galilee called Jesus of Nazareth but often referred to as Messiah, and those interested in his fate were motivated by reasons as different as were their connections with him. The Roman Guard wanted no trouble in or out of the fortress—a public disturbance during the Passover could cost them their heads. The Jewish leaders wanted him put to death. The peculiar powers manifested by the carpenter, who was also a Rabbi, and his extraordinary hold upon the crowds that flocked to hear him preach had at first only filled the leaders with scorn but scorn had turned into fear. They intended to have him removed from the scene even as a memory. The vagrants hanging outside the court were interested in whichever of the parties to a case would call for their services. They were prepared to stir themselves into a frenzy, shout above any din and even break up the court proceedings if sufficiently paid to do so. They were interested in themselves, not in the prisoner. Far from the fortress, desperately wanting the prisoner to be released but not brave enough to say so, were those who had called themselves his disciples. Although they had witnessed the arrest in the garden of

Gethsemane, they could not understand how it had happened or why, and now they did not dare venture out into the streets.

Pilate, urgently awakened in the small hours of Friday, had gone with his retinue to the Fortress, reassuring his wife that the case was routine. She, about to resume her sleep, remembered that by Jewish Law no person could be tried, sentenced or executed on a Sabbath and therefore the prisoner's fate would have to be settled before noon that day.

On the Pavement which was the court of law, the prisoner stood alone amid the jeers of his enemies. Herod had found him innocent earlier that night and had sent him to Pilate who held the final word. At Passover the Jews had the right to ask for the release of a prisoner of their choice which was regarded as irrevocable even by the Romans. The only other prisoner being held at that time was Bar-Abbas, a murderer sentenced to die and, some said, a traitor as well.

As the carpenter's trial got under way not a voice was raised in his behalf or in defense of truth. Where were the blind to whom he had restored sight, the maimed and sick he had made whole, the lepers he had cleansed, the demon-possessed he had set free? Where were the joyous pilgrims who had escorted him into Jeruselem the previous Sunday, waving olive branches and shouting "Hosanna!"? Not one person spoke for the prisoner except a woman who was not even present at the trial. A woman not of his own people who probably had never even seen him. She was Pilate's wife whose concern was not so much the prisoner as her husband's conscience.

Not long after the Governor had donned his robes and left the palace, Claudia awoke suddenly from an uneasy second sleep and, as if a light had flashed upon her memory, recalled the dream that had startled her back to consciousness. It was about the prisoner. Losing no time, she summoned a trusted servant and sent him flying across town to the Fortress with a message to be delivered to no one but the Governor himself.

Pilate, facing the noisy crowd from his high seat, let the house servant approach and listened intently as the man repeated the words which Claudia had committed to his memory: "Have nothing to do with that innocent man; I was much troubled on his account in my dreams last night." Pilate knew that such a warning from his wife must not go unheeded. Moreover her obvious concern for his well-being strengthened him against a mob which was becoming more hostile the more he pressed for justice. Having found no substance in the charges brought against Jesus of Nazareth, he was convinced that the jealous Jewish hierarchs had brought him to trial for spite. Besides, like most people of his time, he believed in dreams and he fully trusted Claudia's intuition.

The loud cries in the court, which subsided while the messenger came and went and Pilate pondered, suddenly rose again to a menacing pitch. Pilate was determined to release the prisoner. Knowing himself to be a master in the art of crowd manipulation, he was confident that even at Passover he could impose his will upon the Jews.

As soon as Pilate had appeared in court the crowd had shouted: "Release Bar-Abbas! Crucify Jesus!" and the cry went up again each time the Governor loudly asked the question: "Why crucify Jesus? What wrong has he done?" Fortified by Claudia's message he was increasingly convinced that he could sway the fickle populace and in accordance with the law he repeated his question a third time: "Why Crucify Jesus? What wrong has he done?" The mob, egged on by the high priests, was unrelenting, yelling louder and louder: "Release Bar-Abbas! Crucify Jesus!"

Pilate, now standing erect and stern before the mob, was about to defy their yells and pronounce his own decision when a voice soared above the din stating clearly: "If you let this man go, you are no friend to Caesar!" The unexpected dart hit home. The vision of an angry Emperor rose before Pilate's eyes. The power he held from Caesar was suddenly at stake. He could face no such risk. He paused, took water and in the sight of Jesus and the crowd washed his hands saying: "My hands are clean of this just man's blood. See to that yourselves." A roar of triumph went up. Then a crisp order outshouted the roar: *"Ite, tenete eum."* The commander of the Roman Guard had pronounced the mandatory fatal words: "Go! Take him away!" And they took Jesus away.

Pontius Pilate departed from the Fortress, his duty done. The Nazarene would be crucified, but not by the will of Rome. Rome, through him, had publicly washed its hands of the case. He would tell Claudia exactly how he had tried to save the prisoner by declaring his innocence and how at the last moment his power had been threatened, forcing him to yield to the will of the dangerous mob. For her sake, however, as well as for Rome and himself, he had come out of it with clean hands and although Claudia's warning had failed to save a life it had at least salvaged a principle of justice. Pilate must have felt certain that the Passover feast with its rituals and celebrations would quickly expunge the incident from public memory. He was proved wrong.

The Gospel does not reveal the content of Claudia's dream about the "innocent man" that troubled her so intensely as to force her into immediate action, but its significance is emphasized by the mere fact of its being reported. History shows that Jews, Romans, Christians and countless other people all over the globe, believing in the divine origin of dreams, have not dared ignore their message or their warnings. However, if the purpose of Claudia's dream was that of saving the prisoner, why did its divine originators not send it to an influential Jew who could have, if he wished, stood in court to speak the truth? Or why not to Pilate himself? Instead it troubled the sleep of a woman who was not Jewish and may not even have known the prisoner's name but who, believing in justice as much as she believed in her husband, became determined to save a just man's life and a judge's conscience from the burden of an irreparable error.

The wording of her message showed her love for Pilate and also made him aware that she knew her limitations. She said: "Have nothing to do with that innocent man", thus letting her husband know at once that her prime concern was for him. She might have said: "That man is innocent, you must save him", which would have been tantamount to telling a judge how to pass judgment. Such foolish audacity on her part might well have angered Pilate or aroused his jealousy. He might have wondered what the prisoner was to his wife that she made such a plea for his discharge. But Claudia allowed her sensitivity and her intuition to guide her choice of words so that suddenly Pilate felt her at his side, giving him support because she understood the problem he was facing.

There can hardly have been any direct connection between Jesus and the Roman Governor's wife, but the strange occurrence which linked them for one tragic fleeting moment is replete with meaning. One cannot, of course, read into it a role which Jesus himself assigned through her to women of another age, yet Claudia is the one woman highlighted in the Gospel only because she was a wife—a woman cast in a role she could not have played in any other guise. Therefore the manner in which she used her position in behalf of Jesus, albeit indirectly, has a great deal to say to any wife who, like Claudia, cares about her husband but also cares about principles.

There are contemporary Claudias and Pilates all about us who, without the rank or attributes of their Roman predecessors, respond to motivations very similar to theirs. The modern counterpart of Pilate could be any man of influence in whatever field of endeavor who is ready to abide by honesty and justice so long as his delegated power is not placed in jeopardy. The modern Claudia, wife of this influential man, would dread the possibility that some day she might see him forfeit conscience and principle for the sake of power. If that day came would she, like Pilate's wife, dare to intervene?

On that fateful Friday two thousand years ago, Claudia was responding to a challenge thrown to her conscience by her moral equality with man. Being a Roman, she was legally and otherwise regarded as a complete person equal to her husband in most respects and not his chattel as were the Hebrew women of her time. Claudia measured herself with Pilate not in terms of power or rank, but in terms of the human values in which their personal relationship was grounded. Evidently she felt that equality gave her not merely the right but also the duty of safeguarding these values if she saw them endangered. When something as vital as her husband's conscience was caught in a struggle between principle and power, she threw herself to the side of principle, offering Pilate a shield against the assaults of vested power. The power she feared that day was that of the Jewish leaders who, on the eve of Passover, would certainly be in court to influence the people's demand for the release of a prisoner. But she had not forseen or reckoned with the power of a blackmailer who, suddenly voicing a threat to Pilate's seemingly impregnable position, could score a victory as ignoble as it was swift.

Like countless twentieth century women married to government officials serving on foreign soil, Claudia was well prepared for her share of the formal duties that went with her husband's post. However, she obviously did not consider her role fulfilled once she had met her social obligations. Her concern was of a more enduring substance. Having recognized the pitfalls that inevitably surrounded her husband's status as it soared, she had learned to combine intuition with common sense in trying to steer him away from danger. Evidently, she also had thoroughly appraised his qualities as well as his faults—among which arrogance seems to have been notable—and knew how to deal with both. She must have gained Pilate's confidence as well as his respect as a loyal and intelligent partner else she would not have dared send him a messenger as he sat in judgment in the Fortress. He probably regarded her as his eyes and ears, knowing he could trust her evaluation of what she saw and heard. But, with it all, Claudia sensed just how far she could go and in this lay much of her success.

If in our minds we remove this scene from its setting in Jerusalem some twenty centuries ago, divesting Pilate and Claudia of their uncommon and exalted status, while leaving the basic issue unchanged, we may plausibly imagine a judge of any modern court finding himself under political pressure to declare right what he knows to be wrong and wrong what he knows to be right. Determined as he is to stand by the truth and justice his conscience dictates, a blackmailer suddenly insinuates a threat to his reputation and his power. Not daring to risk an open confrontation with a dishonest enemy, he struggles with himself but finally his conscience yields like Pilate's. His bench is saved and justice appears to have been served, whereas in fact innocence has paid full price. Instead of a law court, the locale might be a bank, a business office, a school, a government bureau or any 'seat of power' however minor where dishonesty will dare to ply its trade, counting on the vulnerability of a conscience forced to vie with the lure of that power. When Pilate was caught in such a contest Claudia rushed in to bolster his conscience, expecting its full weight to be pulled for justice.

As with Pontius Pilate, the moment of decision is not shared. It is the loneliest of all human acts, for it is in the secrecy of conscience that every individual makes ultimate choices to which only truth is witness. When conflict develops, the inner force of conscience striving to push outward is challenged by outer forces pushing inward through the channel of the mind. No human being alive has escaped this inner confrontation regardless of how trivial or how grave the case may be. It could be that of a small child trying to fight back the temptation of the cookie jar—he has promised not to open it but his mind assures him that nobody will ever know if he does it carefully! It could be the case of Pilate whose conscience said 'this man is innocent and must be saved' but whose mind insisted 'if you save his life you will forfeit your power and be disgraced.'

Conscience knows what is right yet is not always strong enough to resist the pressure of a mind bent on a different course. Conscience must then receive support, but only one who understands its workings can provide it. Claudia knew how to reach Pilate's conscience and the washing of his hands proves that she did. Even if one firmly believes that the final outcome of Jesus' trial was determined not by men but by the will of God, the significance of Claudia's efforts remains unchanged. She acted as a partner in the union of two minds using her powers to 'reach in' as a complement to Pilate's 'reaching out'. She is also a reminder that conscience and justice exist universally above race, creed, nationality or sex. In fact Claudia who was Latin by race, pagan by religion, Roman by nationality and a woman took up the cudgels for justice in defense of a man who was a Semite by race, a monotheist and a Rabbi, and Hebrew by nationality. Although Jesus was put to death, his innocence was publicly declared mainly because of her. She won a victory for the principle of Justice by forcing it to be placed in the limelight. For this she earned a place in history and in the Gospel.

On a less exalted plane than that of sheer principle, Claudia has much to say to wives striving for equality within the marriage compact. Pilate's reaction to her message in such a critical situation demonstrates the level of equality she had attained. As we know, the laws and mores of Rome gave her considerable independence as well as equality, but being intelligent she must have realized that equality of mind, mutual respect and trust cannot be legislated or made customary. These are conquests which every individual must achieve according to his or her aspirations and potential.

It is interesting to consider how Claudia developed her part of the relationship of minds that seems to have existed in her marriage. The scant picture we get of her in the Gospel is nonetheless sufficient to let us surmise more than we can see. To begin with, she cannot have been a nagging wife. Most of these are motivated by selfishness and it was certainly not for egotistic motives that Claudia warned her husband. Rightly or wrongly she believed in Pilate's integrity and was committed to helping him to protect and to preserve it. In modern times the integrity of any man in business, a profession or public life is constantly pressured by the emphasis on status and possessions as marks of his success. Covetous wives who nag their husbands to enable them to keep abreast of their wealthier neighbors are responsible for the tragic end of many a brilliant career. The downhill glide usually begins when the husband commits his first and very minor breach of honesty to satisfy his wife's absurd requests. Other breaches almost inevitably follow until the name of them is crime that shatters lives, wrecks families and destroys achievement. Had such wives seen marriage as a partnership designed not for the purpose of climbing social ladders or scaling the peaks of affluence but rather to safeguard, enhance and enjoy the integrity of enduring values, their husband's consciences would not have been subjected to an erosion they proved unable to arrest. Obviously not every nagging or covetous woman forces her husband into an illegal path, but the persistent repetition of her complaints excludes her from his confidence and makes it easier for him to resort to any measure that promises to satisfy her.

Claudia was a woman of religious faith since she believed in dreams as a manifestation of the will of the gods whose commands she obeyed. She was resourceful and a quick thinker as her instant despatching of the messenger reveals. She had enough common sense to word her message so that it could be easily memorized. If, as one may well suspect, it was spelled out for her by her own intuition, there was virtue in not altering it under the influence of probable second thoughts.

Would that we knew how she reacted to Pilate's account of how the case against the Nazarene had ended. The washing of his hands and the public proclamation by his own words of the prisoner's innocence may have preserved her trust in him. At all events we know that she was still gallantly at his side some time later when he was suddenly recalled to Rome, but not for the death of Jesus which had been considered a minor incident by the leading Jews, the putting away of potentially dangerous subversive. The blunder that plunged Pilate into obscurity was the massacre of a throng of Samaritans protesting not against the rule of Rome but against the arrogance of the Imperial representative, Pilate himself, who had dared to break a religious law. There is no record that Claudia on this occasion tried to stay his hand. She was probably unaware of it until after the deed had been done. But she remained loyal to Pilate nonetheless, revealing what must have been another of her characteristic traits.

All told, it is only a glimpse that we have of Claudia and of her marriage with Pilate, as she fleetingly comes into the orbit of Jesus the Nazarene a few hours before his death. Yet even from this glimpse, as from the brief encounters between Jesus and other women, there emerge signals and guideposts reaching out beyond the limitations of time and place that are too valuable to be ignored by any wife who cares enough to look for them with the eyes of her heart and mind.

11

The Voice at Dawn

"Mary!" the cherished voice suddenly spoke her name as she stood weeping in the garden, a step away from the entrance to the cave in which the body of Jesus had been buried. Hardly daring to believe her ears yet absolutely certain of who had called her, she thrust out her hand to touch the figure outlined in the pale light of the dawn while the cry of "Master!" escaped joyously from her lips. But Jesus stopped her gesture mid-air saying: "Do not touch me. I have not yet ascended to the Father. But go to my brothers and tell them that I am now ascending to my Father and your Father, my God and your God."

Then as unexpectedly as he had appeared he was gone. For a moment Mary stood transfixed, still holding the basket of spices and perfumed oils she had brought to embalm the Master's body. She looked over her shoulder to the empty tomb, turned again towards the trees that seemed to have absorbed the beloved figure, then ran to deliver his stupendous message to the disciples. She wanted to laugh for the sheer joy of having seen him again and also to cry because he was no longer there.

The sun had not yet risen in the sky and not a person was out on the road. As Mary alternately ran and walked, her breath short less from exertion than from astonishment, all that had happened in the previous thirty-six hours came back to her as clearly as if she were living it for the first time. She realized that the tiny band of heartbroken followers of the Nazarene who had remained as near as they could be to the foot of the cross had consisted of four women and only one man—John, the Nazarene's youngest and dearest disciple. The women had been Mary, mother of Jesus, Salome, mother of John, Mary, mother of James and Joseph and she, Mary of Magdala. She knew that Peter, the disciple who had not fled as did all the others when Jesus was apprehended in the garden of Gethsemane, was now somewhere in seclusion, burning with remorse for his threefold denial. Nine of the eleven were hiding in fear. John on Golgotha with the women was concerned with Mary of Nazareth who had refused to abandon the small corner of stony ground on which she sat as near the cross as she was allowed. Huddling together, the other three women had suppressed any display of grief lest the guards who wanted no problems force them into silence or remove them from the hill. Never ceasing to love the Master and to believe in him, every second of his agony had also been their agony. But she, Mary of Magdala, loved him with a pervading ardor and her despair had been almost beyond endurance as she helplessly watched him die. Yet she had not flinched, her tragic eyes riveted on the bleeding face until the end.

Finally when it was over, John had led Mary, the mother, away to some place where she would be safe and cared for. But she, Mary of Magdala, had stayed on the hill of death and Mary, the mother of James, also with her until Joseph of Arimathaea had come to claim the body for burial in his own tomb. Wrapping the body of Jesus in a sheet, Joseph had taken it away and the two women following him had seen "where they laid him." Then they hastened home to the city because the Sabbath which started at sundown was almost upon them, demanding twenty-four hours of inactivity and seclusion. But no sooner had the sun set on the Saturday than Mary Magdalene, Mary the mother of James and Salome went out to buy spices and herbs and whatever else they needed to anoint the body as the last tribute of their love and respect. With outward calm they blended the spices and herbs and prepared the aromatic unguents in order to be ready to start out for the tomb before the dawn of Sunday.

Joanna, wife of Chuza a steward in Herod's house, was accompanying Mary Magdalene and the mother of James as they left the house to steal through the chilly semidarkness of the city's lower quarters, making their way to the city gates and to the sepulchre beyond the walls. Their main preoccupation had been the stone, Mary of Magdala clearly remembered. On Friday she and Mary had seen it rolled against the entrance to the cave. Its size was imposing. Although each of them wondered apprehensively how they would get it moved, they went on their way undeterred.

Mary Magdalene shivered as she recalled the shock of seeing the cave open and the stone gone from its entrance. Relieved by the fact but terrified by not knowing how it had come about, they had all peered inside the tomb and seen a youth clad in white sitting on the right-hand side who exclaimed: "Fear nothing; you are looking for Jesus of Nazareth who was crucified. He has risen; he is not here; look, there is the place where they laid him. But go and give this message to the disciples and to Peter: 'He will go on before you into Galilee and you will see him there, as he told you.' " Totally bewildered, they had taken each other by the hand and run all the way back to the city without exchanging a single word. To the eleven men who were now all together in hiding, they had faithfully reported what they had seen and what they had been told to say, but the disciples did not believe them.

Nevertheless Peter and John decided to go to the tomb and John, the younger of the two outdistancing the other, reached the sepulchre first. Peering in he saw the linen wrappings lying there, but did not enter. Peter did go into the cave and saw the folded linens and also the napkin which had been placed over the face of Jesus, rolled and set in a place by itself. John, taking courage from Peter, also went in and suddenly believed. The two men returned to the city, but Mary Magdalene who had followed them, unable to tear herself away from the place that even so briefly had sheltered the beloved Master's body, remained in the garden wondering dejectedly how she could find that body.

Looking once again inside the tomb she had seen two figures in white sitting one at the head and one at the foot of the niche where the body had lain. They had not been there when John and Peter had visited the place only minutes before. One of the white-clad figures, seeing the tears in her eyes, had asked her solicitously why she was crying. She had answered: "They have taken my Lord away and I do not know where they have laid him". As she was about to turn around to leave the tomb, a voice, not very distinct because it was outside, asked the same question: "why are you weeping?" Stepping out and thinking the questioner was a gardener, she said: "If it is you, sir, who removed him, tell me where you have laid him and I will take him away."

It was then that the unmistakable voice called her name: "Mary!" and she recognized Jesus standing within reach of her hand! As she tried to touch him he interrupted her gesture, then he bade her take a message to the disciples.

Even as she hurried to fulfill his command the vision of Jesus was still before her eyes, his person as real as he had ever been in life! Quickly she blurted out to the men: "I have seen the Lord! I have seen the Lord!" and gave them his message. Her shattering experience bore witness to one of the most moving and beautiful episodes in the Gospel, even as it was the first announcement of what was to become a central fact of Christian faith: Jesus had risen from the dead!

It cannot have been mere happenstance that the bearing of this crucial message—the announcement of the Master's resurrection—fell to the lot of a woman. No more than it had been happenstance that the woman of Samaria was sent to tell her men that the Jew who had spoken to her at Jacob's Well was the long-awaited Messiah. It is not reasonable to ignore the fact that the two great cornerstones of Christian faith—that Jesus of Nazareth was the Messiah and that he rose again from the dead—were each first revealed to a woman who, as the Nazarene's appointed messenger, was sent to disclose it to her men. The Samaritan woman, a stranger to Jesus and inimical to his people, was sent to convey the news among strangers. Mary of Magdala, one of the Master's most faithful followers, a woman of his own race and a native of his region, was sent to convey the news to his intimates. Thus it was by the word of a woman that tidings so fundamental in Christianity were made known to persons representing the two extremes of a spectrum of local relationships, symbolic of relationships in the world as whole: the enemies and the friends.

As the Nazarene's existence approached its end, the part he caused woman to play at his side revealed ever more clearly the pattern he had followed persistently in regard to her from the miracle of Cana to the miracle outside the empty tomb. He treated every woman with the consideration due to an equal and he always cast light upon the qualities and talents he considered as being more typical of woman than of man. When his end had come it was at his place of burial that he raised woman's role to its loftiest height. Here he revealed to Mary of Magdala that he had conquered death. Here, by calling her name, he linked the conclusion of his terrestrial mission with the rise of a spiritual force offering redemption and peace to all humanity.

Who was this Mary upon whom so much attention is focused by the Gospels as they record the forty dreadful hours that elapsed between the planting of the ignominious cross with its innocent victim upon the desolate summit of Mount Golgotha, and the calling of her name by the risen Jesus in the peaceful garden near the place of burial? In the pale translucence of the dawn the call had ushered in a new day, a day without precedent and never to be repeated, a day which for twenty centuries has shined its light into the souls of uncounted millions of believers around the world.

She was young and beautiful this Mary, known as Magdalene from the town of Magdala where she was born on the shores of the Galilean sea. In the Middle Ages a false legend began to spread that she had been a woman of ill repute. Absolutely nothing substantiates this charge, whereas it is told in the Gospels that she suffered from a nervous disorder ascribed in her day to possession of her soul by the devil. Its manifestations, known to us today as epileptic seizures, left her body without vitality and her mind in shatters. Jesus cast "out of her seven devils", although we have no exact account of when he cured her. Her sense of relief and liberation must have been wonderful beyond description.

She may first have seen Jesus as he walked by the water's edge, alone with his thoughts, or in the company of a few friends. Did she plead for his help or did he invite her to join his followers? Was it her eyes, betraying her fear of the evil force within her, that touched the heart of the Nazarene? This we can only guess, but we know that the beauty of her spirit and the generosity of her heart, buried until then, burst forth to inflame her undying love for the Rabbi of Nazareth who had saved her. What more perfect recipient of such love could she have found than Jesus? From him who was love incarnate, she reaped incalculable rewards.

There was in Mary of Magdala, as in the other three women who went with her to Mount Golgotha on that fateful Friday, an extraordinary measure of physical as well as moral courage. Is there a difference between the forms which courage takes in men and women? On that occasion there must have been since every man who had protested his undying devotion to the Master promptly abandoned him to his fate when the metal of the soldiers' lances glimmered in the torchlight in Gethsemane. One among them, true enough, did vehemently try to protect the Master by striking a soldier with his blade and cutting off his ear. But when Jesus restored the ear, thus barring all further show of violence, even that disciple lost his nerve and fled. That those men loved the Nazarene cannot be denied, therefore does their cowardice mean that a man's love is different from the love of a woman? Even on Golgotha that afternoon there were lances held menacingly by soldiers who used them to prevent the crowd from demonstrating for or against the executions. The women of Jesus forced themselves to be still, restrained their weeping so as not to provoke the guards and never abandoned the heart-rending scene. Above all it took incredible fortitude to witness the agony of a loved one to the end yet they and John were the only friends who did.

Mary of Magdala had been their leader on Golgotha and at the tomb. She seems to have taken the initiatives. The Gospels mention her name fourteen times in this one dramatic episode and usually before the names of other persons with her. From the record we perceive her to have been poised and practical in her decisions which demonstrates that recovery from her possession or nervous condition had been complete. Her vision of Jesus in the garden was certainly not, as some critics have suggested, the invention of a paranoic but the very real experience of a mystic or of a psychic which she may well have been. It was not long after the disciples had received the announcement of the Master's resurrection from Mary that he appeared to them and later to others in Galilee. Thus Mary Magdalene became one of several who saw the risen Lord, but she had been the first!

That Jesus chose to make a woman the first witness to his resurrection was the most dramatic confirmation of his belief in her spirituality. Being his last direct encounter with a woman, this was also his final effort to persuade man to recognize and honor the dignity of woman, her intellectual capacity and her equality with him as a full-fledged person. He entrusted her with the most significant message of his mission on earth—that he had overcome death—and in so doing paid the highest tribute to her faith and to her love. Above all he held her up as the person most worthy of his trust. He must have felt entirely certain that Mary of Magdala would not only accept the vision of him as a reality but also that nothing would deter her from sharing her conviction and her joy with the disciples. He probably suspected that they would not believe her for, despite the three years they had spent at his side and witnessed his regard for women, they were still influenced by the rules of their society. Woman being chattel could not bear witness in a court of law or in any other place. Here was Mary of Magdala, a young woman profoundly enamored of the Master, coming to bear witness to an event without precedent and beyond the pale of reason! Although the refusal to accept her testimony did occur, Jesus must also have known that Mary of Magdala would not become doubtful herself because of it, or be hurt by the disciples' disbelief or cease to hold fast to her report. The

Magdalene fulfilled all of the Master's expectations and in fact did not hesitate to return with the doubting men to the deserted burial cave.

It would be interesting to know what she thought they would find when they reached the garden other than the empty tomb. Mary knew that Jesus would not be there to bear her out and the deserted niche did not constitute evidence that the Master's body was alive elsewhere! Such probable thoughts failed to affect her belief or her courage in facing a possible charge of lying to the disciples. Truth prevailed even in the absence of Jesus or of other proof of his resurrection, and both disciples were irresistibly moved to accept the woman's testimony.

To some extent the women of the time of Jesus were confronted with obstacles to the recognition of their equality similar to those which confront modern woman in her struggle to obtain a broader and more complete social equality than Jesus sought for the women of Israel. Legal inequities, traditions, mores and most importantly the habit of centuries had to be proved wrong and destroyed. In Israel Jesus was a single voice more often than not crying in the wilderness. But there can be no doubt that his major purpose was achieved for the community of his followers did admit, almost from the start of his mission, that woman was endowed with a soul as was man. His struggle in woman's behalf was centered on this point, knowing as of course he did, that if he could convince woman herself that she had a soul, he would have endowed her with a source of power which no person or rule or law could take from her.

He restored to woman full mastery over her inner self by showing her how to discover her own spiritual riches, how to increase them and how to use them. This primary purpose of his emerges clearly out of each of his encounters with a woman whose 'faith' he always praises, making it the justification for whatever "good thing" comes to her through him. It may be her health restored, her conscience pacified, a loved one brought back from the dead that is the woman's tangible gift of grace from the Nazarene, but these are always second to her faith and always derived from it.

By convincing her, as indeed he sought to convince all his followers men and women alike, that faith is the secret treasure and inviolable possession of every human creature which can be destroyed or diminished only with the owner's acquiescence, he taught woman to be the mistress of her will to act and of the spiritual power motivating her will. Mary of Magdala is the most brilliant example of a woman who, enslaved not only by the inequities of society but also by a derangement of her mind, once restored to mental normalcy by his miraculous touch gives evidence through her courage, leadership and poise of the irresistible power generated within her by her own liberated soul.

Modern woman may not aspire to a vision of the risen Jesus, she may not be in an anguished quest for a vanished body, or in other ways affected by the conditions Mary of Magdala had to struggle with, but her problems are frequently just as overwhelming as were Mary's. In our time we do not hear of people being possessed by the devil as was Mary, but Jesus may well have singled out the Magdalene for her unique role precisely because she had to come back to normalcy from so far. This must certainly offer an added measure of encouragement to normal women who without Mary's initial handicap seem unable to find their spiritual identity or to attain spiritual liberation. Basically the answer to this quest was found by the Magdalene in the giving of herself and of her goods to the cause of Jesus and through him to others she could also serve. This is likewise true of all of the Nazarene's followers who soon discovered that all they had was what they had given and what they gave was returned multiplied a hundredfold. It was Mary of Magdala who received the greatest gift in return for her love: she heard the voice of Jesus speak her name although she knew beyond the possibility of doubt that his voice had been silenced by his death upon the cross. She saw him stand before her, shrouded in light and filled with life, although she knew that his body, tightly wrapped in burial linens, had been sealed in a tomb behind a colossal stone.

Mary of Magdala plays such a significant role in the Gospel narratives that more has been conjectured about her than about most of the other women followers of Jesus. Because she was young, beautiful and well-to-do and because she was close to the Master, she aroused jealousy in people with small minds in and out of his circle or from her home town which Jesus apparently never visited. The label of a redeemed sinner has clung to her name to the extent of becoming synonymous with Magdalene. In reality Jesus did not set her free from a life of sin but from the possession of the devils.

She was more a woman of action than a contemplative such as Mary of Bethany whom Jesus praised for choosing this way, yet in the end the Magdalene's reward was far more exalted than any which the other Mary is known to have received. Did Jesus mean to suggest that he rated activism higher than meditation? The answer to this question seems to emerge from a comparison one may draw between Martha and Mary of Bethany on the one hand and Mary of Magdala on the other. Each of the sisters was a woman of faith but Martha was preponderantly an activist and largely a homemaker and Mary was preponderantly a thinker and a mystic. In Mary of Magdala there seems to have been a balanced measure of activism, faith and mysticism. Perhaps therefore we must conclude that the final glorious encounter between Jesus and the Magdalene is intended to point her out to all women as an example of womanhood that came the closest to perfection.

Certainly if the commission given by Jesus to woman or, to put it differently, the role he saw for her in any and every society was one of 'inreach', his revelation of himself to Mary and his message for the disciples which he entrusted to her add new depth to the meaning of that word. Is there a lesson to womankind to be seen in her stoic endurance of the indescribable torment of heart and mind it must have been for her who loved him to see Jesus slowly pass away in torture before her eyes? She stayed quietly until the end giving us the measure of her loyalty. Yet she was quick to take action, wasting no time in following those who carried his lifeless body to the tomb and leading her elder female companions to purchase the items needed for anointing the poor mangled body. Lastly she chose to remain alone beside the empty tomb when the other faithful who had come to view it had departed in puzzlement and fear. These were the manifestations of her activism. Her stoicism at the foot of the cross belonged to the part of her that was courage and will-power. The contemplative in her, resorting to prayer and meditation must have prevailed over the stressful Sabbath, between the crucifixion and resurrection, when silence and stillness enslaved the world around her. The mystic, perhaps even the psychic and above all the soul pervaded by faith, ready to perceive a vision beyond the sight of human eyes, was the innermost Mary of Magdala whose exultant spirit could cry out to the disciples: "I have seen the Lord! I have seen the Lord!"

There is need for women such as she in today's world. Women who can bring out of their own depths the activism, the meditative and the mysticism the seeds of which are dormant in every human being. But when Jesus sent the Magdalene, as he had once sent the Samaritan, to be his messenger to men, he was making it unmistakably clear that humankind is a partnership and that sharing is its lifeline. Whatever Jesus gave to woman, be it confirmation of his own mission expressed by the word Messiah, be it the revelation of a portent such as his return from the dead, the gift was not for her alone. It was for all mankind of which she represented only half. Her duty was to share it with the men and to make it acceptable by virtue of her own understanding of its value. The men's part was then to carry the gift further by their own particular power of outreach, by their own particular activism and their own particular spiritual drive.

12

Carrying On

Towards evening of that overwhelming Sunday which in the Christian calendar is called Easter, the small circle of Jesus' friends had all come together in one place. The prevailing mood was indescribable composed as it was of joy because the Master was alive after all, of disbelief because to speak of rising from the dead was absurd, of fear because the body might have been stolen by spiteful enemies who might now track down the disciples and do away with them as well. Each one had his own explanation none sufficiently convincing to swing the lot to his side. The women were also in that room, Mary the mother of Jesus among them with John faithfully at her side.

Cloepas and one other of the faithful had arrived late and breathless telling of how, as they were going towards Emmaus earlier that afternoon, a stranger had joined them and, staying with them to have supper on the road to Jerusalem, had blessed the bread as he broke it. Suddenly they had recognized Jesus and almost as suddenly he had vanished. Simon Peter also had seen him that afternoon, all of which confirmed what Mary of Magdala had first reported. Then, without warning, "as they were all talking about this, there he was, standing among them. Startled and terrified they thought they were seeing a ghost . . . for it seemed too good to be true." But Jesus ate a piece of fish they had cooked to prove that he was made of flesh and bones and talked to them a while concluding: "I am sending upon you my Father's promised gift; so stay here in this city until you are armed with power from above."

For forty days Jesus continued to appear among them, a presence even more vital than when he had been on earth, stretching their minds that they might grasp the scope of the mission on which they were about to embark. After that the twelve disciples—Matthias replacing Judas—dispersed in all directions far beyond the confines of their native land. Several women accompanied them implementing the partnership of hearts and minds inspired by the Nazarene. Others who had never known Jesus joined them as they traveled, testifying to the persuasive power which already emanated from the very presence of the apostles. They became among the most vital supporters of the new Christian communities.

Some of these we know by name, Lydia, Priscilla, Phoebe and Dorcas among them, women who surrendered their lives to the redemptive flame ablaze within them. Lydia, a business woman in the city of Philippi in Macedonia, now a part of Bulgaria, became the first Christian convert in all Europe. The question, 'Was this happenstance?' again beggars the answer. Born in Thyatira, today's Akhisar, Turkey, she moved to Philippi as a young woman and established a trade in purple dyes, one of the costliest products of her time. Only the Roman officials, the nobility and the rich could sport that striking color in their garments or in the hangings in their palaces. Successful and respected as Lydia was in business, she was a woman in whom the concerns of the spirit took precedence over all others. She and many of her male and female workers belonged to a group of Jews who with unfailing regularity met to pray on the banks of the river. Apparently a few among them had heard Jesus preach in Jerusalem and had told their friends about his teachings.

Paul, on his first visit to Philippi with Timothy and Silas, sensing that they were on fertile soil for their missionary work, soon discovered the Jewish prayer group who welcomed his eloquence at their meetings. This was the core of the first Christian community. Lydia, a leading force, was the first to be baptized on European soil. Accommodating Paul and his companions in her spacious house, she enabled them to open up the meeting place that cradled the first Christian church on the continent. The business ability, by virtue of which Lydia had amassed considerable wealth, was matched in her by an irresistible spiritual drive. She organized such large and enthusiastic public gatherings to hear the word of Jesus preached by Paul that they disturbed the Roman authorities. Breaking them up with their soldiery, the Romans threw scores of converts into jail as well as Paul and his companions. When they were released by a converted jailer it was in Lydia's house that their injuries were treated and they well cared for until they could depart in safety. Those who had not been baptized received the cleansing sacrament which united them all in a new brotherhood.

In Philippi's society which did not regard women as chattel Lydia had imposed herself as the equal of man in a world of traders, but as such she remained a rare exception. Nevertheless the unique combination of business acumen and deep spirituality converted not only her workers and her household but a number of her influential clients as well. The Philippian church grew strong. Once Paul and his companions had departed they apparently never saw Lydia again but Paul, aware of how stupendously she served the cause of Jesus, wrote to her saying: "I thank my God upon every remembrance of you, always in every prayer of mine for you all." With her at his side he had laid the cornerstone of Christendom in Europe.

Lydia speaks to women of any age or society who like her have a respected place in a profession or a trade as well as an inner life, inviting them to use their prestige to open the minds of those around them to the riches of the spirit. Like the women who met the Nazarene in person, she who only knew him in her mind had the courage of her convictions and practiced what she believed. Her example at Philippi opened doors into the realm of the spirit for countless men and women who had never known that such a stupendous experience could be theirs.

It was in Corinth that Paul discovered Priscilla who taught the gospel of Jesus. She and her husband, Aquila, a tent-maker like Paul, were Jews banned from Rome by an edict of the Emperor Claudius, their status as Jews having been further endangered by their conversion to Christianity. Paul came upon this remarkable couple in a Corinthian synagogue where on a Sabbath they were teaching the doctrine of Jesus and making converts even as they spoke. Mothers, convinced by the eloquence of Priscilla, became her ardent followers and in turn converted their own husbands and children.

The opposition the couple had already aroused as they went about the city preaching was aggravated by the presence with them of Paul who was finally haled into court. However, the Roman magistrate before whom he appeared had secretly become a convert himself and therefore heard the case only to dismiss it. Soon afterwards Aquila and Priscilla found it advisable to leave Corinth and, following Paul, went to Ephesus where they immediately resumed their proselytizing in the synagogue and in the streets. It was from Paul's pen that they received their highest commendation, in his letter to the church of Rome in which he placed the name of Priscilla before that of Aquila, indicating that of the two teachers she was the more effective.

On his way to Ephesus, Paul stopped at Cenchreae, the port of Corinth, which had a growing Christian community. Here he entrusted his letter to the Romans to a woman named Phoebe, who thus became his personal representative to the Christians in the Imperial city which he had not yet visited. Little is known about Phoebe, her occupation if any or her family, but she appears to have been a woman of sufficient means to be able to travel to such distant places as Rome. In Cenchreae she had a house similar to the one Lydia had at Philippi and just as hospitable. The converts gathered there and those who were in need of assistance were never left uncared for or wanting.

For all this Paul was grateful and said so in his letter to the Romans in these words: "She has herself been a good friend to many, including myself." He also added a phrase mentioning her position in the church and revealing the esteem in which she was held. He wrote: "I commend to you Phoebe, a fellow-Christian who holds office in the congregation at Cenchreae. Give her, in the fellowship of Christ, a welcome worthy of God's people and stand by her in any business in which she may need your help." This proves how close was this woman's association with the work of the apostle, how much he relied on her cooperation, how completely he trusted her judgment and her faith. In the case of Phoebe as in that of Lydia and Priscilla, we see the partnership of the first men and women followers of Jesus already in full swing.

One fact which emerges clearly from what we know of Lydia, Priscilla and Phoebe is that, while the disciples had learnt directly from Jesus to regard woman as their equal and make her their partner, these women themselves must have contributed something so valuable to the partnership that the disciples came to consider it indispensable. We know that these were all competent women, and all inflamed by total dedication to their new faith. Far from trying to imitate the men who had become their companions they proved to possess abilities usually associated only with men, as, for instance, in business and industry. But they impressed the men as invaluable assets for the Christian cause also because they made them aware of certain aspects of the feminine mind and personality which most men, apparently, had not observed. Because they were, in some respects different they provided a complement and a balance to the attributes of the male.

A woman who enriched the early Christian community with her intelligent approach to charity was Dorcas who, in the cosmopolitan city of Joppa, made her mark as a leading citizen by engaging in a most feminine pursuit: needlecraft. Raised where poverty was visible and it is in most seaports and not a woman of great wealth herself, she gave generously of her time, skill and substance to its alleviation. She was wont to purchase large quantities of cloth and to make them into garments for the poor. To be sure that her aid went where it was most needed, she took time to look into the appeals that came to her, to call personally on widows and bereaved families and to find homes for orphaned children.

Partly because of her compassionate heart, but even more because of her constructive notion of 'doing good' and her way of investigating needy cases without hurting the sensitivities or casting umbrage on the pride of those appealing for help, the councils of the Christian churches and communities held her membership in great account. Her name was known even to the disciples who had never met her or been to Joppa. Thus when the report of her death and an urgent call for his presence reached Peter who was preaching at Lydda, he set out for the coastal city without delay. A vast assembly of weeping people who had been aided by Dorcas met him at the city gates, leading him to where the body of their benefactress was laid out for burial.

Asking to be left alone with her, Peter prayed a long time. Finally, perhaps remembering what he had seen Jesus do for the daughter of Jairus, he took Dorcas' hand in his, bidding her rise up. Miraculously the blood resumed its course through the cold body and, opening her eyes, Dorcas saw the apostle who had brought her back to life. The story of her recovery at the hands of Peter spread through Joppa like wildfire, strengthening the faith of those who were already Christians and adding large contingents to their ranks.

But Dorcas had done more than clothe the poor and meet their other needs. It was the spirit in which she served her fellow man that inspired countless other men and women to follow in her wake. In the councils of the new churches on which she sat as their equal, the men valued her judgment, her counsel and her practical wisdom, all seeming to emerge from within an aura of joyful altruism typical of those whom the teaching of Jesus had set afire.

These women who appear in early Christian history among the disciples of Jesus, serving his cause abroad as passionately as if they had known him in his lifetime, have much to say to modern woman. Inflamed by a deep belief and striving for a high goal, they gained prominence as persons companioning the men in spite of the prevailing religious exclusivity, in spite of the inhibiting customs of their society, in spite of traditions which caused them to be treated as the inferiors of man. Their partnership with the disciples took root not because they imitated man or sought to replace him in his tasks, but because they created new tasks which proved to be as indispensable as man's to the attainment of their common goal. Exceedingly important, moreover, is the fact that the men and women of early Christianity, sharing a great faith, drew strength for their several missions and commissions from the power of the spirit. The spirit is an entity upon which neither age nor sex, neither race nor status can leave the mark of their discrimination. The human as well as the purely spiritual cause which they served filled them with such exultation that as mere mortals they found themselves transcending the limitations inflicted upon mortals by such worldly frailties as ambition, thirst for power, lust for possessions, jealousy or distrust. Indeed these ageless barriers to equality are far more difficult to overcome than the overly estimated barrier of sex.

Interestingly enough, while it is from the word of Jesus and from his actions that we gather the strongest testimony to the inherent and fundamental equality of women and men, it is to those of Paul, his most brilliant apostle, that men still turn for proof of woman's inferiority. That fact is that whoever cites Paul in this respect is limited to two passages in his letters, one directed to the churches in Corinth and one to Timothy at Ephesus. The first of these states: "As in all congregations of God's people, women should not address the meeting. They have no license to speak, but should keep their place as the law directs. If there is something they want to know, they can ask their own husbands at home. It is a shocking thing that a woman should address a congregation." To Timothy he wrote: "A woman must be a learner, listening quietly and with due submission. I do not permit a woman to be a teacher, nor must woman domineer over man; she should be quiet." As many a learned scholar has made clear in analyzing these passages which lie at the roots of discrimination against women in Christian churches and are used to justify it, conditions prevalent in Paul's time in both Corinth and Ephesus are a fundamental cause of his restraints on women. In both these cities which were centers of thriving pagan cults, the young Christian churches had been joined by temple harlots and by priestesses devoted to the orgiastic rituals performed in honor of Diana, Dionysus and other gods. These women added the loudness of their pagan forms of worship to those practiced by the Christians, scandalizing them and giving rise to dissension in the congregations. In writing as he did to the Corinthians and to Timothy for the Ephesians on the subject of women in their respective churches, Paul was establishing a rule of conduct designed to differentiate true Christian women from those who were so only by their use of the name. Otherwise how could he have praised Priscilla for her public preaching and teaching, Lydia or Phoebe for their action in Church Councils?

Although Paul remained proud of his Jewish heritage, he accepted and faithfully practiced the teachings of Jesus, abandoning his obsolete traditional stance under their influence. That his attitude towards women was deeply altered from what it had been before his own conversion is proven by his equal acceptance of all Christian followers and by his association with those who labored together to propagate the new faith, be they women or men.

In our time, especially in the Western world, the equality of men and women in Church life, in the hierarchy or in the priesthood, has become an issue of deep concern in and out of religious circles. It is second only to the basic issue of woman's equal rights in finding employment, pursuing careers, receiving remuneration or earning promotions as well as her right to equal status with man in seeking and holding public office. Unfortunately even in the more advanced societies of the West these aspects of equality are still far from being attained.

However, the principle matter of concern for those who wish to see woman as the full and true partner of man is another. It is the necessity that woman herself be aware of the distinction between being 'equal' or being 'identical' with man. She cannot be identical with man anymore than he can be identical with her because nature has decreed otherwise in certain vital respects and because when two different beings try to become identical one must inevitably become an imitation if not a travesty of the other. Equality is achieved only between individuals who are totally genuine, for they alone can recognize the value of their genuine diversities.

With today's growing male awareness of what the feminine dimension can offer to the management of society in spiritual, intellectual and practical terms, men who hold the power which women ought to share have little use for women who strive to think, act, react or look like them. Modern society is in need of moral influences, psychological approaches and intellectual perceptions that are new, in that they have never yet been tested in seeking solutions to problems by which all of humanity is now affected. The only possible source for such new forces is womankind because, be it repeated, in a bisexual world she is man's only peer.

Even a generalized assessment of the spiritual, psychological and intellectual attributes which may be described as feminine because they are and always have been common to women in general, must of necessity fall short of being either accurate or complete, as also would the assessment of similar attributes commonly described as masculine. Nonetheless woman's 'diversities' can be noted, even so briefly, to good advantage for the cause of feminism and partnership.

To begin with, woman, excluded by the very supremacy of man, from most power struggles to which he has been subjected from time immemorial, has retained a scale of values that tends to make her more rapidly aware of the moral and social aspects of many a situation than of its material ones. For the same reason, as well as by virtue of the fact that woman tends to heed her instinct or intuition more than most men, her judgments and decisions are influenced rather by an elemental sense of justice and of compassion than by more tangible or more profitable considerations. The world's average woman is to some degree endowed with a special capacity for selflessness which reaches its highest point in motherhood but is frequently manifested in women who have never borne a child. Thus she will resort to actions that appear to defy logic or elementary concepts of safety because she believes them to be necessary to the well-being or to the life of someone other than herself. In material ways, woman in general tends to be more conservative than acquisitive and less wasteful of resources than the male whose faith in his own ability to increase, multiply or transform matter at his will tends to make him extravagant in the use of it.

Motherhood, which universally identifies woman with all women, makes her less chauvinistic than man and more inclined to look for what human beings have in common rather than for what separates them. Usually endowed with an 'other' sense by which she vicariously lives the experiences of those she loves, feeling as they feel, knowing what troubles them, she invigorates them with her own strength. Sometimes this 'other' sense will spur her as it did Claudia, Pilate's wife, to make decisions with seemingly little justification but which prove to be right. To heed the counsel of this 'sense' usually demands a form of courage bordering on apparent rashness yet sustained by faith.

Woman's faith, whatever its form, be it religious or humanistic, be it in God or in people or in both, is not essentially deeper or more abiding than man's, but it is to woman a more intimate reality than it is to most men. Her acceptance as true and real of much that lies beyond the purview of the physical senses tends to make her pursue rather than recoil from manifestations of the spiritual and the supernatural. In the framework of pure religious faith, from the early days of the Christian church, woman has demonstrated her capacity to achieve unsurpassed heights of mysticism.

Spirituality, even if latent rather than manifest, is an intrinsic part of woman's nature. Perhaps this is because her body is constructed to harbor another body which, in turn, becomes the harbor for another spirit. Or perhaps it is because, in the primordial society and forever thereafter, even though increasingly in symbolic form, man is the builder and defender of the hearth and woman the custodian of its flame. She, closer to the natural elements of fire and water, lighting one, carrying the other; he coming to grips with the outside world, provider as well as defender, challenged by the necessity of survival for himself, for her and for their young, spurred by the eagerness to advance, conquer and leave a heritage to those who follow. Yet without the water she carried he could not have lived and without the flame she kept alight he could not have found his way home. Perhaps in this was rooted man and woman's first complete and pervading partnership. Primitive and uncomplicated, its imperative was survival.

With survival came progress, a compound of inequities, a force moving faster and faster, pushing humanity on and on, from age to age, fitfully, creating gaps and pitfalls as well as stupendous heights, undeterred by the better or the worse. Now, eons and eons of time beyond the primordial society, when man has taught himself to set foot on the moon and to whirl through the firmament chasing planets and stars, that first imperative confronts society once again, still primitive and stark: again, it is survival.

The basic fact of it has not changed since the beginning but everything around it has. How to retrieve the assurance of survival for a world which man has made capable of total self-destruction is not a problem. It is an enigma. That first elementary partnership of minds matching, for directness of purpose, the partnership of bodies, has been dwarfed out of existence. It did not grow with progress, thus allowing man to be the predominant when not the exclusive manager of human affairs. His failure to ensure survival, now so brutally revealed, is a sin of omission rather than commission. He has not scrimped on time or talent in making gigantic conquests in science and technology, in agriculture and industry, in economics and even in education. But he has not known how to foresee the human and social problems that such ravenous progress would inevitably create. Once the problems were evident he failed to arrest their growth. He has no solutions that take humanity itself into prime account, having long overlooked the fact that progress must be at the service of humanity, not humanity at the service of progress.

The demands made upon man as single manager of human affairs by progress on the one hand, which dies if it pauses, and by humanity on the other, which needs to pause lest it die, were too disparate for him to meet or apparently even to fully comprehend. Progress is a matter of 'reaching out'. Solving the human problems generated by it is a matter of 'reaching in'. In a world which is fundamentally and inescapably bisexual, it ought to have become clear that the management of its affairs needs likewise to be bisexual. The equal partnership of minds with man and woman sharing the total burden by dividing the task between them according to their inborn talents, now cries for recognition as the best, perhaps the only instrument potentially capable of ensuring survival.

Woman's awareness of her power, lying dormant through the ages, is now awake, and the call for her rightful equality with man no longer falls on deaf ears. Now is the time to drive beyond equality to take on the challenge of full-fledged partnership with man. Indeed the challenge is not to her alone. It confronts both sexes demanding equally from each a broader vision, a sharpened intelligence, more concern for human affairs and, most important, a new measure of self-discipline: for woman in taking on responsibilities she has never held before, for man in relinquishing responsibilities he has never shared before. How shall they be shared? Logically woman should take those which man has fulfilled poorly or not at all in facing the human problems generated by the progress he has distributed so unevenly to the world. Thus the imaginary dividing line which must not actually divide should fall between the 'outreach' and the 'inreach', those vast areas of human life to which the respective special talents of either man or woman are more keenly attuned.

To Jesus of Nazareth, be he seen as divine or human but in all cases a compassionate revolutionary, our own anguished age owes the light he focused on woman's innate capacity for 'reaching in' and on man's for 'reaching out'. By his own declaration to his disciples, he commissioned man to preach and to exemplify his doctrine to the far ends of the world. Woman, instead, he commissioned by the unmistakable implications of his personal encounters with her to restore and strengthen the moral and spiritual foundations of society, that his redemptive doctrine might rest securely upon them. Man's 'outreach' has not failed entirely since

Ms. Theresa Girard
29806 Spring River Dr
Southfield, MI 48076

TEACH
TOLERANCE

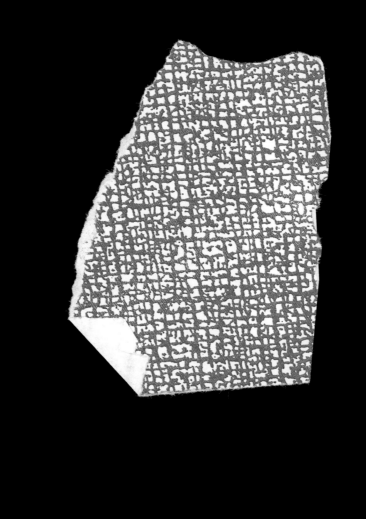

there is now no part of the world to which the Christian message has not been delivered. However, in the course of nearly twenty centuries, where the message has been accepted, the practice has increasingly fallen short of the doctrine. Persistently woman has been denied the right to fulfill her own commission outside the narrow limits of her home and even there obliged to recognize the superior authority of man.

Although titular Christians have never been a majority in the world and are now less than one fourth of its inhabitants, they control a vast majority of power and, until recently, of world resources as well. Tragically enough, history shows that more wars and violent revolutions, more repression of human rights, more wanton destruction of human lives and public assets have been dispensed to mankind by the 'Christian civilization' of the West in the last two thousand years, than had ever happened on such a scale before the preaching of Christian doctrine. Thus, as we contemplate growing starvation, maldistribution of wealth and resources, agitation of peoples rightly resentful of a miserable lot, mal-treatment of the environment, ongoing production of lethal super-weapons and the threat of life's annihilation on this planet, all wrapped within a declining morality, we recognize that the mission of 'outreach' alone, intended to enrich humanity with a doctrine of love and redemption, has indeed failed.

In the final analysis it is in woman that humanity must place its hope of survival through a restoration of universal moral values, of decency and of love practiced instead of mouthed. Therefore, to have perceived through the words and actions of Jesus of Nazareth his appraisal of woman and of her role in society, will at least have placed in sharp relief the fact that in his eyes *woman is the equal of man.*

As to the facets of woman's role in partnership with man, emerging from the Nazarene's encounters with his women followers and also with Mary his mother, their applicability to universal woman is self-evident as is their relevance to woman's life in our time. Pieced together, these facets form a pattern wherein woman stands in command of attributes of intellect and spirit with which nature has endowed her, as it has endowed man with his, of equal value yet not identical.

During the boyhood of Jesus, when it was Mary's responsibility to raise him, his relationship to his mother cannot obviously be defined as an encounter into which Jesus placed the implications of a role for her to play. Nonetheless the way in which Mary fulfilled the responsibilities of motherhood has much to say to young mothers who, by observing Jesus the man cannot fail to perceive the quality of his upbringing.

At Cana, instead, the encounter between Mary and Jesus was not so much one between mother and son as it was one between adults concerned with the well-being of their fellow humans. Here, by being persuaded to grant Mary's request, Jesus implicitly demonstrated the power of a woman's altruism and of her understanding of human frailties. The sick woman, healed near the Sea of Galilee, owed her recovery to a faith which, over the years, had kept alive her persistent determination to overcome her disease. The Samaritan woman at the well was invited by Jesus to break down a racial barrier despite the law which supported it, because he believed her capable of summoning sufficient courage to choose the law of God against the law of man. And he had judged her correctly.

Saving the life of an adulteress, he taught woman how to deal with human moods when he transformed the anger of a crowd into harmless curiosity. When he praised Mary of Bethany's dedication to the things of the mind and spirit, he made woman aware of the riches of her intellect and of her right to develop them. And although he reproached Martha for fussing too much over household chores, he rewarded the stalwart faith lying beneath her endless activitism when he raised her brother Lazarus from the dead.

Aware that woman, poor or rich as she may be, is usually the holder of the family purse, he praised the woman who found her lost coin, making all women realize the power which came to them through this trust and, even more, by fulfilling it with meticulous care. To balance the material implications of his praise, he exalted the spiritual value of a materially insignificant gift contributed by a poor widow to the alms-box at the Temple.

The meaning and the implications of hospitality in which woman has an outstanding part, he highlighted in praising two women for gestures which men had censured as extravagant. One of these women, Mary of Bethany who, like the nameless woman of Galilee, had anointed him with costly oils, he immortalized for the prophetic significance of her act. To all women he was saying that the gift of prophecy, prescience or premonition is to be cherished and cultivated. Woman must use it as she would the gift of an exceptional singing voice which must be trained and disciplined in order to achieve its true potential.

The power of moral suasion that a wife can exercize upon a husband she loves, shines forth from the effort made by Pilate's wife to save the life of Jesus. Regardless of its outcome, the role she played must make every wife aware of her right or duty to try to protect the conscience of her husband when she knows it to be vulnerable to temptation. That a force beyond her control defeated her effort in no way diminished its merit.

The love of Mary Magdalene, so persistent, so loyal and so brave, cannot fail to strike responsive chords in any woman's heart. She testifies to how a desperately grieving woman is capable of weathering a crisis with quiet wisdom, intelligent decisions and outward calm through the stabilizing power of her love. Radiating from her, this love comforted and reassured those who grieved and trembled with her. The mystic quality of her faith found a stupendous reward in the vision which revealed the power of the spirit to overcome the finality of death.

The picture of universal woman, equal partner of universal man, is thus before us as a composite of the women who were briefly encircled by the radiance of the Nazarene. His light shows us her inner qualities more clearly than her outer skills, for it is her gifts of mind and spirit that make her partnership with man more indispensable now than ever before to the recovery of a sickened society if not, indeed, to its survival. The concerned woman does not have to be a Christian or a religiously inclined person to recognize the relevance to our time of the Nazarene's belief in the equality of woman and in her power.

A scholar and a preacher of this century, Julius Mark, having defined Jesus "the greatest of all teachers and the kindliest of all men" added this: "For Christians, Jesus was born divinely and lived humanly. For Jews, he was born humanly and lived divinely." Whether we believe Jesus to have been God or man, we know how deeply he loved and understood humanity. Two thousand years ago his mission was to redeem and renovate society by redeeming and renovating the human beings who constitute it. He showed them a way to go and a goal to strive for, men and women moving together, 'reaching in' and 'reaching out'.

If the dangers which pervade today's world are to be fought off, neither man nor woman can afford to ignore their mounting threat. With their diversities complementing one another and their similarities enhancing their common strengths, man and woman together may well succeed in so repairing our damaged planet and in so improving the lot of its inhabitants that survival may be assured. The challenge to woman is a double one. Like man, she must do her part, whatever the cost, but she must also raise her sights. She can no longer limit her goal to being recognized as man's equal in a society of his making. She must become his complete and equal partner because, by nature's irrevocable dictate, she is his only peer.

For those who choose to see it, a light emanates from the teaching and actions of Jesus of Nazareth to illumine a pattern for woman's striving and to offer a promise of fulfillment.

APPENDIX

The Gospel Citations

*The Gospel citations which follow are taken
from THE NEW ENGLISH BIBLE, published jointly by the
University Presses of Oxford and Cambridge in 1961.*

2

"Now it was the practice of his parents to go to Jerusalem every year for
the Passover festival; and when he was twelve, they made the pilgrimage
as usual. When the festive season was over and they started for home,
the boy Jesus stayed behind in Jerusalem. His parents did not know of
this; but thinking that he was with the party they journeyed on for a
whole day, and only then did they begin looking for him among their
friends and relations. As they could not find him they returned to Jerusalem to look for him; and after three days they found him sitting in the
temple surrounded by the teachers, listening to them and putting questions;
and all who heard him were amazed at his intelligence and the answers he
gave. His parents were astonished to see him there, and his mother said to
him, 'My son, why have you treated us like this? Your father and I have
been searching for you in great anxiety.' 'What made you search?' he said.
'Did you not know that I was bound to be in my Father's house?' But they
did not understand what he meant. Then he went back with them to
Nazareth, and continued to be under their authority; his mother treasured
up all these things in her heart. As Jesus grew up he advanced in wisdom
and in favour with God and men."

LUKE 2:42

3

"On the third day there was a wedding at Cana-in-Galilee. The mother of
Jesus was there, and Jesus and his disciples were guests also. The wine
gave out, so Jesus's mother said to him, 'They have no wine left.' He

answered, 'Your concern, mother, is not mine. My hour has not yet come.' His mother said to the servants, 'Do whatever he tells you.' There were six stone water-jars standing near, of the kind used for Jewish rites of purification; each held from twenty to thirty gallons. Jesus said to the servants, 'Fill the jars with water', and they filled them to the brim. 'Now draw some off', he ordered, 'and take it to the steward of the feast'; and they did so. The steward tasted the water now turned into wine, not knowing its source; though the servants who had drawn the water knew. He hailed the bridegroom and said, 'Everyone serves the best wine first, and waits until the guests have drunk freely before serving the poorer sort; but you have kept the best wine till now.'

This deed at Cana-in-Galilee is the first of the signs by which Jesus revealed his glory and led his disciples to believe in him."

JOHN 2:1

4

"Then a woman who had suffered from haemorrhages for twelve years came up from behind, and touched the edge of his cloak; for she said to herself, 'If I can only touch his cloak, I shall be cured.' But Jesus turned and saw her, and said, 'Take heart, My daughter; your faith has cured you.' And from that moment she recovered."

MATTHEW 9:20

"As soon as Jesus had returned by boat to the other shore, a great crowd once more gathered around him . . . Among them was a woman who had suffered from haemorrhages for twelve years; and in spite of long treatment by doctors, on which she had spent all she had, there had been no improvement; on the contrary, she had grown worse. She had heard what people were saying about Jesus, so she came up from behind in the crowd and touched his cloak; for she said to herself, 'If I touch even his clothes, I shall be cured.' And there and then the source of her haemorrhages dried up and she knew in herself that she was cured of her trouble. At the same time Jesus, aware that power had gone out of him, turned round in the crowd and asked, 'Who touched my clothes?' His disciples said to him, 'You see the crowd pressing upon you and yet you ask, "Who touched me?" Meanwhile he was looking round to see who had done it. And the woman, trembling with fear when she grasped what had happened to her, came and fell at his feet and told him the whole truth. He said to her, 'My daughter, your faith has cured you. Go in peace, free forever from this trouble.' "

MARK 5:21

"Among them was a woman who had suffered from haemorrhages for twelve years; and nobody had been able to cure her. She came up from behind and touched the edge of his cloak, and at once her haemorrhage stopped. Jesus said, 'Who was it that touched me?' All disclaimed it, and Peter and his companions said, 'Master, the crowds are hemming you in and pressing upon you!' But Jesus said, 'Someone did touch me, for I felt that power had gone out from me.' Then the woman, seeing that she was detected, came trembling and fell at his feet. Before all the people she explained why she had touched him and how she had been instantly cured. He said to her, 'My daughter, your faith has cured you. Go in peace.' "

LUKE 8:43

5

". . . Jesus set out once more for Galilee. He had to pass through Samaria, and on his way came to a Samaritan town called Sychar, near the plot of ground which Jacob gave to his son Joseph and the spring called Jacob's well. It was about noon, and Jesus, tired after his journey, sat down by the well.

The disciples had gone away to the town to buy food. Meanwhile a Samaritan woman came to draw water. Jesus said to her, 'Give me a drink.' The Samaritan woman said, 'What! You, a Jew, ask a drink of me, a Samaritan woman?' Jesus answered her, 'If only you knew what God gives, and who it is that is asking you for a drink, you would have asked him and he would have given you living water.' 'Sir', the woman said, 'you have no bucket and this well is deep. How can you give me "living water"? Are you a greater man than Jacob our ancestor, who gave us the well, and drank from it himself, he and his sons, and his cattle too?' Jesus said, 'Everyone who drinks this water will be thirsty again, but whoever drinks the water that I shall give him will never suffer thirst any more. The water that I shall give him will be an inner spring always welling up for eternal life,' 'Sir,' said the woman, 'give me that water, and then I shall not be thirsty, nor have to come all this way to draw.'

Jesus replied, 'Go home, call your husband and come back.' She answered, 'I have no husband.' 'You are right', said Jesus, 'in saying that you have no husband, for, although you have had five husbands, the man with whom you are now living is not your husband; you told me the truth there.' 'Sir,' she replied, 'I can see that you are a prophet. Our fathers worshipped on this mountain, but you Jews say that the temple where God should be worshipped is in Jerusalem.' 'Believe me,' said Jesus, 'the time is coming when you will worship the Father neither on this mountain, nor in Jerusalem. You Samaritans worship without knowing what you worship, . . . the time approaches, indeed it is already here, when those who are real worshippers will worship the Father in spirit and in truth . . . God is spirit, and those who worship him must worship in spirit and in truth.' The woman answered, 'I know that Messiah . . . is coming. When he comes he will tell us everything.' Jesus said, 'I am he, I who am speaking to you.'

At that moment his disciples returned, and were astonished to find him talking with a woman; but none of them said, 'What do you want?' or, 'Why are you talking with her?' The woman put down her water-jar and went away to the town, where she said to the people, 'Come and see a man who has told me everything I ever did. Could this be the Messiah?' They came out of the town and made their way towards him. . . . Many Samaritans of that town came to believe in him because of the woman's testimony . . .''

JOHN 4:3

6

"At daybreak [Jesus] appeared again in the temple, and all the people gathered round him. He had taken his seat and was engaged in teaching them when the doctors of the law and the Pharisees brought in a woman detected in adultery. Making her stand out in the middle they said to him, 'Master, this woman was caught in the very act of adultery. In the Law Moses has laid down that such women are to be stoned. What do you say about it?' They put the question as a test, hoping to frame a charge against him. Jesus bent down and wrote with his finger on the ground. When they continued to press their question he sat up straight and said, 'That one of you who is faultless shall throw the first stone.' Then once again he bent down and wrote on the ground. When they heard what he said, one by one they went away, the eldest first; and Jesus was left alone, with the woman still standing there. Jesus again sat up and said to the woman, 'Where are they? Has no one condemned you?' 'No one, sir', she said. Jesus replied, 'No more do I. You may go; do not sin again.' "

JOHN 7:53, 8:1-11

7

"While they were on their way Jesus came to a village where a woman named Martha made him welcome in her home. She had a sister, Mary, who seated herself at the Lord's feet and stayed there listening to his words. Now Martha was distracted by her many tasks, so she came to him and said, 'Lord, do you not care that my sister has left me to get on with the work by myself? Tell her to come and lend a hand.' But the Lord answered, 'Martha, Martha, you are fretting and fussing about so many things; but one thing is necessary. The part that Mary has chosen is best; and it shall not be taken away from her.' "

LUKE 10:38-42

". . . Bethany was just under two miles from Jerusalem, and many of the people had come from the city to Martha and Mary to condole with them on their brother's death. As soon as she heard that Jesus was on his way, Martha went to meet him, while Mary stayed at home.

Martha said to Jesus, 'If you had been here, sir, my brother would not have died. Even now I know that whatever you ask of God, God will grant you.' Jesus said, 'Your brother will rise again.' 'I know that he will rise again', said Martha, 'at the resurrection on the last day.' Jesus said, 'I am the resurrection and I am life. If a man has faith in me, even though he die, he shall come to life; and no one who is alive and has faith shall ever die. Do you believe this?' 'Lord, I do', she answered; 'I now believe that you are the Messiah, the Son of God who was to come into the world.'

With these words she went to call her sister Mary, and taking her aside, she said, 'The Master is here; he is asking for you.' When Mary heard this she rose up quickly and went to him. Jesus had not yet reached the village, but was still at the place where Martha left him. The Jews who were in the house condoling with Mary, when they saw her start up and leave the house went after her, for they supposed that she was going to the tomb to weep there.

So Mary came to the place where Jesus was. As soon as she caught sight of him she fell at his feet and said, 'O sir, if you had only been here my brother would not have died.' When Jesus saw her weeping and the Jews her companions weeping, he sighed heavily and was deeply moved. 'Where have you laid him?' he asked. They replied, 'Come and see, sir.' Jesus wept. The Jews said, . . . Could not this man, who opened the blind man's eyes, have done something to keep Lazarus from dying?'

Jesus again sighed deeply; then he went over to the tomb. It was a cave, with a stone placed against it. Jesus said, 'Take away the stone.' Martha, the dead man's sister, said to him, 'Sir, by now there will be a stench; he has been there four days.' Jesus said, 'Did I not tell you that if you have faith you will see the glory of God?' So they removed the stone.

Then Jesus looked upwards and said, 'Father, I thank thee: thou hast heard me. I knew already that thou always hearest me, but I spoke for the sake of the people standing around, that they might believe that thou didst send me.'

Then he raised his voice in a great cry: 'Lazarus, come forth.' The dead man came out, his hands and feet swathed in linen bands, his face wrapped in a cloth. Jesus said, 'Loose him; let him go.' "

JOHN 11:17

"When Jesus arrived at the president's house and saw the flute-players and the general commotion, he said, 'Be off! The girl is not dead: she is asleep'; but they only laughed at him. But, when everyone had been turned out, he went into the room and took the girl by the hand, and she got up. The story became the talk of all the country round."

MATTHEW 9:23

"While he was still speaking, a message came from the president's house, 'Your daughter is dead; why trouble the Rabbi further?' But Jesus, over-hearing the message as it was delivered, said to the president of the synagogue, 'Do not be afraid; only have faith.' After this he allowed no one to accompany him except Peter and James and James's brother John. They came to the president's house, where he found a great commotion, with loud crying and wailing. So he went in and said to them, 'Why this crying and commotion? The child is not dead: she is asleep.' But they only laughed at him. After turning all the others out, he took the child's father and mother and his own companions and went in where the child was lying. Then, taking hold of her hand, he said to her *'Talitha cum'*, which means, 'Get up, my child.' Immediately the girl got up and walked about —she was twelve years old. At that they were beside themselves with amazement. He gave them strict orders to let no one hear about it, and told them to give her something to eat."

MARK 5:35

"When Jesus returned, the people welcomed him, for they were all expecting him. Then a man appeared—Jairus was his name and he was president of the synagogue. Throwing himself down at Jesus's feet he begged him to come to his house, because he had an only daughter, about twelve years old, who was dying. And while Jesus was on his way he could hardly breathe for the crowds.

. . . While he was still speaking, a man came from the President's house with the message, 'Your daughter is dead; trouble the Rabbi no further.' But Jesus heard, and interposed, 'Do not be afraid,' he said; 'only show faith and she will be well again.' On arrival at the house he allowed no one to go in with him except Peter, John and James, and child's father and mother. And all were weeping and lamenting for her. He said, 'Weep no more; she is not dead: she is asleep.' But they only laughed at him, well knowing that she was dead. But Jesus took hold of her hand and called her: 'Get up, my child.' Her spirit returned, she stood up immediately, and he told them to give her something to eat. Her parents were astounded; but he forbade them to tell anyone what had happened."

LUKE 8:40

8

"Once he was standing opposite the temple treasury, watching as people dropped their money into the chest. Many rich people were giving large sums. Presently there came a poor widow who dropped in two tiny coins, together worth a farthing. He called his disciples to him. 'I tell you this,' he said: 'this widow has given more than any of the others; for those others who have given had more than enough, but she, with less than enough, has given all that she had to live on.' "

MARK 12:41

"In the hearing of all the people Jesus said to his disciples: 'Beware of the lawyers who love to walk up and down in long robes, and have a great liking for respectful greetings in the street, the chief seats in our synagogues, and places of honour at feasts. These are the men who eat up the property of widows, while they say long prayers for appearance' sake; and they will receive the severest sentence.

He looked up and saw the rich people dropping their gifts into the chest of the temple treasury; and he noticed a poor widow putting in two tiny coins. 'I tell you this,' he said: 'this poor widow has given more than any of them; for those others who have given had more than enough, but she, with less than enough, has given all she had to live on."

LUKE 20:45-21:1

9

"One of the Pharisees invited him to dinner; he went to the Pharisee's house and took his place at table. A woman who was living an immoral life in the town had learned that Jesus was dining in the Pharisee's house and had brought oil of myrrh in a small flask. She took her place behind him, by his feet, weeping. His feet were wetted with her tears and she wiped them with her hair, kissing them and anointing them with the myrrh. When his host the Pharisee saw this he told himself, 'If this fellow were a real prophet, he would know who this woman is that touches him, and what sort of woman she is, a sinner.' Jesus took him up and said, 'Simon, I have something to say to you.' 'Speak on, Master', said he. 'Two men were in debt to a money-lender; one owed him five hundred silver pieces, the other fifty. As neither had anything to pay with he let them both off. Now, which will love him most?' Simon replied, 'I should think the one that was let off most.' 'You are right,' said Jesus. Then turning to the woman, he said to Simon, 'You see this woman? I came to your house; you provided no water for my feet; but this woman has made my feet wet with her tears and wiped them with her hair. You gave me no kiss; but she has been kissing my feet ever since I came in. You did not anoint my head with oil; but she has anointed my feet with myrrh. And so, I tell you, her great love proves that her many sins have been forgiven; where little has been forgiven, little love is shown.' Then he said to her, 'Your sins are forgiven.' The other guests began to ask themselves, 'Who is this, that he can forgive sins?.' But he said to the woman, 'Your faith has saved you; go in peace.' "

LUKE 7:37

"Jesus was at Bethany in the house of Simon the leper, when a woman came to him with a small bottle of fragrant oil, very costly; and as he sat at table she began to pour it over his head. The disciples were indignant when they saw it. 'Why this waste?' they said; 'it could have been sold for a good sum and the money given to the poor.' Jesus was aware of this, and said to them, 'Why must you make trouble for the woman? It is a fine thing she has done for me. You have the poor among you always; but you will not always have me. When she poured this oil on my body it was her way of preparing me for burial. I tell you this: wherever in all the world this gospel is proclaimed, what she has done will be told as her memorial.' "

MATTHEW 26:6

"Jesus was at Bethany in the house of Simon the leper. As he sat at table, a woman came in carrying a small bottle of very costly perfume, oil of pure nard. She broke it open and poured the oil over his head. Some of those present said to one another angrily, 'Why this waste? The perfume might have been sold for thirty pounds and the money given to the poor'; and they turned upon her with fury. But Jesus said, 'Let her alone. Why must you make trouble for her? It is a fine thing she has done for me. You have the poor among you always, and you can help them whenever you like; but you will not always have me. She has done what lay in her power; she is beforehand with anointing my body for burial. I tell you this: whenever in all the world the Gospel is proclaimed, what she has done will be told as her memorial.' "

MARK 14:3

"Six days before the Passover festival Jesus came to Bethany, where Lazarus lived whom he had raised from the dead. There a supper was given in his honour, at which Martha served, and Lazarus sat among the guests with Jesus. Then Mary brought a pound of very costly perfume, oil of pure nard, and anointed the feet of Jesus and wiped them with her hair, till the house was filled with the fragrance. At this, Judas Iscariot, a disciple of his—the one who was to betray him—said, 'Why was this perfume not sold for thirty pounds and given to the poor?' He said this, not out of any care for the poor, but because he was a thief; he used to pilfer the money put into the common purse, which was in his charge. 'Leave her alone', said Jesus, 'Let her keep it till the day when she prepares for my burial; for you have the poor among you always, but you will not always have me.' "

JOHN 12:1

10

"While Pilate was sitting in court a message came to him from his wife: 'Have nothing to do with that innocent man; I was much troubled on his account in my dreams last night.'

Meanwhile the chief priests and elders had persuaded the crowd to ask for the release of Bar-Abbas and to have Jesus put to death. So when the Governor asked, 'Which of the two do you wish me to release to you?', they said, 'Bar-Abbas.' 'Then what am I to do with Jesus called Messiah?' asked Pilate; and with one voice they answered, 'Crucify him!' 'Why, what harm has he done?' Pilate asked; but they shouted all the louder, 'Crucify him!'

Pilate could see that nothing was being gained, and a riot was starting; so he took water and washed his hands in full view of the people, saying, 'My hands are clean of this man's blood; see to that yourselves.' And with one voice the people cried, 'His blood be on us, and on our children.' "

MATTHEW 27:19-25

"From that moment Pilate tried hard to release him; but the Jews kept shouting, 'If you let this man go, you are no friend to Caesar; any man who claims to be a king is defying Caesar.' When Pilate heard what they were saying, he brought Jesus out and took his seat on the tribunal at the place known as 'The Pavement' ('Gabbatha' in the language of the Jews). It was the eve of Passover, about noon. Pilate said to the Jews, 'Here is your king!' They shouted, 'Away with him! . . . Crucify him!' 'Crucify your king?' said Pilate. 'We have no king but Caesar', the Jews replied. Then at last, to satisfy them, he handed Jesus over to be crucified.' "

JOHN 19:12

11

"So the disciples went home again; but Mary stood at the tomb outside, weeping. As she wept, she peered into the tomb; and she saw two angels in white sitting there, one at the head, and one at the feet, where the body of Jesus had lain. They said to her, 'Why are you weeping?' She answered, "They have taken my Lord away, and I do not know where they have laid him.' With these words she turned round and saw Jesus standing there, but did not recognize him. Jesus said to her, 'Why are you weeping? Who is it you are looking for?' Thinking it was the gardener, she said, 'If it is you, sir, who removed him, tell me where you have laid him, and I will take him away.' Jesus said, 'Mary!' She turned to him and said, 'Rabbuni!' (which is Hebrew for 'My Master'). Jesus said, 'Do not cling to me, for I have not yet ascended to the Father. But go to my brothers, and tell them that I am now ascending to my Father and your Father, my God and your God.' Mary of Magdala went to the disciples with her news: 'I have seen the Lord!', she said and gave them his message."

JOHN 20:10